From t

Welcome to our extra-special n
astrological forecast which takes y
up to the end of the century on D

our year-ahead guides all the astrological calculations had to be made using tables and a calculator. Today, by the miracle of computers, we have been able to build our knowledge and hard work into a program which calculates the precise astrological aspect for every day in a flash.

When Shakespeare wrote 'The fault, dear Brutus, is not in our stars, but in ourselves', he spoke for every astrologer. In our day-to-day forecasts we cannot hope to be 100% accurate every time, because this would remove the most important influence in your life, which is you! What we can hope to do is to give you a sense of the astrological backdrop to the day, week or month in question, and so prompt you to think a little harder about what is going in your own life, and thus help improve your chances of acting effectively to deal with events and situations.

During the course of a year, there may be one or two readings that are similar in nature. This is not an error, it is simply that the Moon or a planet has repeated a particular pattern. In addition, a planetary pattern that applies to your sign may apply to someone else's sign at some other point during the year. One planetary 'return' that you already know well is the Solar return that occurs every year on your birthday.

If you've read our guides before, you'll know that we're never less than positive and that our advice is unpretentious, down to earth, and rooted in daily experience. If this is the first time you've met us, please regard us not as in any way astrological gurus, but as good friends who wish you nothing but health, prosperity and contentment. Happy 1998-9!

Sasha Fenton is a world-renowned astrologer, palmist and Tarot card reader, with over 80 books published on Astrology, Palmistry, Tarot and other forms of divination. Now living in London, Sasha is a regular broadcaster on radio and television, as well as making frequent contributions to newspapers and magazines around the world, including South Africa and Australia. She is a former President and Secretary of the British Astrological and Psychic Society (BAPS) and Secretary of the Advisory Panel on Astrological Education.

Jonathan Dee is an astrologer, artist and historian based in Wales, and a direct descendant of the great Elizabethan alchemist and wizard Dr John Dee, court astrologer to Queen Elizabeth I. He has written a number of books, including the recently completed *The Chronicles of Ancient Egypt,* and for the last five years has co-written an annual astrological forecast series with Sasha Fenton. A regular broadcaster on television and radio, he has also hosted the Starline show for KQED Talk Radio, New Mexico.

YOUR DAY-BY-DAY FORECAST
SEPTEMBER 1998 – DECEMBER 1999

LEO

SASHA FENTON • JONATHAN DEE

HALDANE • MASON

Zambezi

DEDICATION

For the memory of Gary Bailey, a new star in heaven.

ACKNOWLEDGEMENTS

With many thanks to our computer wizard, Sean Lovatt.

———————————————————

This edition published 1998
by Haldane Mason Ltd
59 Chepstow Road
London W2 5BP

ISBN 1-902463-03-X

Designed and produced by Haldane Mason Ltd
Cover illustration by Lo Cole
Edited by Jan Budkowski

Printed in Singapore by Craft Print Pte Ltd

CONTENTS

AN ASTROLOGICAL OVERVIEW OF THE 20TH CENTURY   6

THE ESSENTIAL LEO   16

YOUR SUN SIGN   19

ALL THE OTHER SUN SIGNS   21

YOU AND YOURS   29

YOUR RISING SIGN   36

LEO IN LOVE   41

YOUR PROSPECTS FOR 1999   43

LEO IN THE FINAL QUARTER OF 1998   46

LEO IN 1999   70

An Astrological Overview of the 20th Century

Next year the shops will be full of astrology books for the new century and also for the new millennium. In this book, the last of the old century, we take a brief look back to see where the slow-moving outer planets were in each decade and what it meant. Obviously this will be no more than a very brief glance backwards but next year you will be able to see the picture in much more depth when we bring out our own book for the new millennium.

1900 – 1909

The century began with Pluto in Gemini and it was still in Gemini by the end of the decade. Neptune started out in Gemini but moved into cancer in 1901 and ended the decade still in Cancer. Uranus started the century in Sagittarius, moving to Capricorn in 1904 and ending the decade still in Capricorn. Saturn began the century in Sagittarius, moving to Capricorn in January 1900 and then through Aquarius, Pisces and Aries, ending the decade in Aries.

The stars and the decade

In general terms, the planet of upheaval in the dynastic sign of Sagittarius with Saturn also in that sign and Pluto opposing it, all at the very start of the century put the spotlight on dynasties, royalty and empires. As Saturn left for the 'establishment' sign of Capricorn these just about held together but as the decade ended, the power and control that these ancient dynasties had were loosening their grip on the developed world of the time. Queen Victoria died in 1901 and her son, Edward VII was dying by the end of the decade, so in Britain, the Victorian age of certainty was already coming to an end. The Boer War was only just won by Britain in 1902 which brought a shock to this successful colonial country.

Pluto in Gemini brought a transformation in methods of communications. It was as Saturn entered the innovative sign of Aquarius that these took concrete and useful form. Thus it was during this decade that the motor car, telephone, typewriter, gramophone and colour photography came into existence. Air travel began in 1900 with the first Zeppelin airship flight, the first powered aeroplane flight by the Wright brothers in 1904 and Louis Blériot's flight across the English Channel in 1909. Edison demonstrated the Kinetophone, the first machine capable of showing talking moving pictures in

1910. Even the nature of war changed as technologically modern Japan managed to fight off the might of the Russian empire in the war of 1904 - 1905.

The Treaty of Versailles, followed by further treaties of Aix and Trianon served to crush the German nation and therefore sow the seeds of the next war.

1910 – 1919

Pluto opened the decade in Gemini, moving to Cancer in 1913. Neptune travelled from Cancer to Leo in September 1914 while Uranus moved out of Capricorn, through Aquarius to end the decade in Pisces. Saturn moved from Aries to Taurus, then to Gemini, back into Taurus, then into Gemini again entering Cancer in 1914, then on through Leo and ending the decade in Virgo.

The stars and the decade

Now we see the start of a pattern. Sagittarius may be associated with dynasties but it is the home-loving and patriotic signs of Cancer and Leo that actually seem to be associated with major wars. The desire either to expand a country's domestic horizons or to protect them from the expansion of others is ruled by the maternal sign of Cancer, followed by the paternal one of Leo. Home, family, tradition, safety all seem to be fought over when major planets move through these signs. When future generations learn about the major wars of the 20th century they will probably be lumped together in their minds - despite the 20-year gap between them - just as we lump the Napoleonic wars together, forgetting that there was a nine-year gap between them, and of course, this long stay of Pluto in Cancer covered the whole of this period.

It is interesting to note that Pluto moved into Cancer in July 1913 and Neptune entered Leo on the 23rd of September 1914, just three of weeks after the outbreak of the First World War. Saturn moved into Cancer in April 1914. Pluto is associated with transformation, Neptune with dissolution and Saturn with loss, sadness and sickness. Many people suffered and so many families and dynasties were unexpectedly dissolved at that time, among these, the Romanov Czar and his family and the kings of Portugal, Hungary, Italy and Germany and the Manchu dynasty of China. America (born on the 4th of July, 1776 and therefore a Cancerian country) was thrust into prominence as a major economic and social power after this war. Russia experienced the Bolshevik revolution during it. As Saturn moved into Virgo (the sign that is associated with health) at the end of this decade, a world-wide plague of influenza killed 20 million people, far more than had died during the course of the war itself.

1920 – 1929

The roaring 20s began and ended with Pluto in Cancer. Neptune moved from Leo to Virgo at the end of this decade and Uranus moved from Pisces to Aries in 1927. Saturn travelled from Virgo, through Libra, Scorpio, Sagittarius and then backwards and forwards between Sagittarius and Capricorn, ending up in Capricorn at the end of 1929.

The stars and the decade

Pluto's long transformative reign in Cancer made life hard for men during this time. Cancer is the most female of all the signs, being associated with nurturing and motherhood. Many men were sick in mind and body as a result of the war and women began to take proper jobs for the first time. Family planning and better living conditions brought improvements in life for ordinary people and in the developed world there was a major boom in house building as well as in improved road and rail commuter systems. The time of lords and ladies was passing and ordinary people were demanding better conditions. Strikes and unrest were common, especially in Germany. As the decade ended, the situation both domestically and in the foreign policies of the developed countries began to look up. Even the underdeveloped countries began to modernize a little. Shortly before the middle of this decade, all the politicians who might have prevented the rise of Hitler and the Nazi party died and then came the stock market crash of 1929. The probable astrological sequence that set this train of circumstances off was the run up to the opposition of Saturn in Capricorn to Pluto in Cancer which took place in 1931. The effects of such major planetary events are often felt while the planets are closing into a conjunction or opposition etc., rather than just at the time of their exactitude.

On a brighter note great strides were made in the worlds of art, music and film and ordinary people could enjoy more entertainment than ever before, in 1929 the first colour television was demonstrated and in 1928 Alexander Fleming announced his discovery of penicillin. At the very start of the decade prohibition passed into US Federal law, ushering in the age of organized crime and as a spin-off a great increase in drinking in that country and later on, all those wonderful gangster films. The same year, the partition of Ireland took place bringing more conflict and this time on a very long-term basis.

1930 – 1939

The 1930s should have been better than the 1920s but they were not. Pluto remained in Cancer until 1937, Neptune remained in Virgo throughout the decade, Uranus entered Taurus in 1934 and Saturn moved from Capricorn through Aquarius, Pisces then back and forth between Aries and Pisces, ending the decade in Taurus.

The stars and the decade
Neptune's voyage through Virgo did help in the field of advances in medicine and in public health. Pluto continued to make life hard for men and then by extension for families, while in the 'motherhood' sign of Cancer. While Saturn was in the governmental signs of Capricorn and Aquarius, democracy ceased to exist anywhere in the world. In the UK a coalition government was in power for most of the decade while in the USA, Franklin Delano Roosevelt ruled as a kind of benign emperor for almost three terms of office, temporarily dismantling much of that country's democratic machinery while he did so. Governments in Russia, Germany, Italy, Spain and Japan moved to dictatorships or dictatorial types of government with all the resultant tyranny, while France, Britain and even the USA floundered for much of the time. China was ruled by warring factions. However, there was an upsurge of popular entertainment at this time, especially through the mediums of film, music and radio probably due to the advent of adventurous, inventive Uranus into the music and entertainment sign of Taurus in 1934.

1940 – 1949
War years once again. Pluto remained in the 'paternal' sign of Leo throughout this decade, bringing tyranny and control of the masses in all the developed countries and also much of the Third World. Neptune entered Libra in 1942, Uranus moved from Taurus to Gemini in 1941, then to Cancer in 1948. Saturn began the decade in Taurus, moved to Gemini, Cancer, Leo and finally Virgo during this decade. The 'home and country' signs of Cancer and Leo were once more thrust into the limelight in a war context. Neptune is not a particularly warlike planet and Libra is normally a peaceable sign but Libra does rule open enemies as well as peace and harmony.

The stars and the decade
To continue looking for the moment at the planet Neptune, astrologers don't take its dangerous side seriously enough. Neptune can use the sea in a particularly destructive manner when it wants to with tidal waves, disasters at sea and so on, so it is interesting to note that the war in the West was almost lost for the allies at sea due to the success of the German U-boats. Hitler gambled on a quick end to the war in the east and shut his mind to Napoleon's experience of the Russian winter. Saturn through Cancer and Leo, followed by the inventive sign of Uranus entering Cancer at the end of

the decade almost brought home, family, tradition and the world itself to an end with the explosions of the first atomic bombs.

However, towards the end of this decade, it became clear that democracy, the rights of ordinary people and a better lifestyle for everybody were a better answer than trying to find 'lebensraum' by pinching one's neighbour's land and enslaving its population. Saturn's entry into Virgo brought great advances in medicine and the plagues and diseases of the past began to diminish throughout the world. Pluto in Leo transformed the power structures of every country and brought such ideas as universal education, better housing and social security systems - at least in the developed world.

1950 – 1959

Pluto still dipped in and out of Leo until it finally left for Virgo in 1957. Neptune finally left Libra for Scorpio in 1955, Uranus sat on that dangerous and warlike cusp of Cancer and Leo, while Saturn moved swiftly through Virgo, Libra, Scorpio, Sagittarius and then into Capricorn.

The stars and the decade

The confrontations between dictators and between dictatorships and democracy continued during this time with the emphasis shifting to the conflict between communism and capitalism. The Korean war started the decade and the communist take-over in China ended it. Military alertness was reflected in the UK by the two years of national service that young men were obliged to perform throughout the decade. Rationing, shortages of food, fuel and consumer goods remained in place for half the decade, but by the end of it, the world was becoming a very different place. With American money, Germany and Japan were slowly rebuilt, communism did at least bring a measure of stability in China and the Soviet Union, although its pervasive power brought fear and peculiar witch hunts in the United States. In Europe and the USA the lives of ordinary people improved beyond belief.

Pluto in Virgo brought plenty of work for the masses and for ordinary people, poverty began to recede for the first time in history. Better homes, labour-saving devices and the vast amount of popular entertainment in the cinema, the arts, popular music and television at long last brought fun into the lives of most ordinary folk. In Britain and the Commonwealth, in June 1953, the coronation of the new Queen ushered in a far more optimistic age while her Empire dissolved around her.

LEO

1960 - 1969

This is the decade that today's middle-aged folk look back on with fond memories, yet it was not always as safe as we like to think. Pluto remained in Virgo throughout the decade bringing work and better health to many people. Neptune remained in Scorpio throughout this time, while Uranus traversed back and forth between Leo and Virgo, then from Virgo to Libra, ending the decade in Libra. Saturn hovered around the cusp of Taurus and Gemini until the middle of the decade and then on through Gemini and Cancer, spending time around the Cancer/Leo cusp and then on through Leo to rest once again on the Leo/Virgo cusp.

The stars and the decade

The Cancer/Leo threats of atomic war were very real in the early 1960s, with the Cuban missile crisis bringing America and the Soviet Union to the point of war. The Berlin wall went up. President Kennedy's assassination in November 1963 shocked the world and the atmosphere of secrets, spies and mistrust abounded in Europe, the USA and in the Soviet Union. One of the better manifestations of this time of cold war, CIA dirty tricks and spies was the plethora of wonderful spy films and television programmes of the early 60s. Another was the sheer fun of the Profumo affair!

The late 1960s brought the start of a very different atmosphere. The Vietnam War began to be challenged by the teenagers whose job it was to die in it and the might of America was severely challenged by these tiny Vietcong soldiers in black pyjamas and sandals. The wave of materialism of the 1950s was less attractive to the flower-power generation of the late 60s. The revolutionary planet Uranus in balanced Libra brought the protest movement into being and an eventual end to racial segregation in the USA. Equality between the sexes was beginning to be considered. The troubles of Northern Ireland began at the end of this decade.

In 1969, Neil Armstrong stepped out onto the surface of the Moon, thereby marking the start of a very different age, the New Age, the Age of Aquarius.

1970 - 1979

Pluto began the decade around the Virgo/Libra cusp, settling in Libra in 1972 and remaining there for the rest of the decade. Neptune started the decade by moving back and forth between Scorpio and Sagittarius and residing in Sagittarius for the rest of the decade. Uranus hovered between Libra and Scorpio until 1975 and then travelled through Scorpio until the end of the decade while Saturn moved from Taurus to Gemini, then hung around the Cancer/Leo cusp and finally moved into Virgo.

The stars and the decade

The planets in or around that dangerous Cancer/Leo cusp and the continuing Libran emphasis brought more danger from total war as America struggled with Vietnam and the cold war. However, the influence of Virgo brought work, an easier life and more hope than ever to ordinary people in the First World. Uranus in Libra brought different kinds of love partnerships into public eye as fewer people bothered to marry. Divorce became easier and homosexuality became legal. With Uranus opening the doors to secretive Scorpio, spies such as Burgess, Maclean, Philby, Lonsdale and Penkowski began to come in from the cold. President Nixon was nicely caught out at Watergate, ushering in a time of more openness in governments everywhere.

If you are reading this book, you may be doing so because you are keen to know about yourself and your sign, but you are likely to be quite interested in astrology and perhaps in other esoteric techniques. You can thank the atmosphere of the 1970s for the openness and the lack of fear and superstition which these subjects now enjoy. The first festival of Mind, Body and Spirit took place in 1976 and the British Astrological and Psychic Society was launched in the same year, both of these events being part of the increasing interest in personal awareness and alternative lifestyles.

Neptune in Scorpio brought fuel crises and Saturn through Cancer and Leo brought much of the repression of women to an end, with some emancipation from tax and social anomalies. Tea bags and instant coffee allowed men for the first time to cope with the terrible hardship of making a cuppa!

1980 – 1989

Late in 1983, Pluto popped into the sign of Scorpio, popped out again and re-entered it in 1984. Astrologers of the 60s and 70s feared this planetary situation in case it brought the ultimate Plutonic destruction with it. Instead of this, the Soviet Union and South Africa freed themselves from tyranny and the Berlin Wall came down. The main legacy of Pluto in Scorpio is the Scorpionic association of danger through sex, hence the rise of AIDS. Neptune began the decade in Sagittarius then it travelled back and forth over the Sagittarius/Capricorn cusp, ending the decade in Capricorn. Uranus moved from Scorpio, back and forth over the Scorpio/Sagittarius cusp, then through Sagittarius, ending the decade in Capricorn. Saturn began the decade in Virgo, then hovered around the Virgo/Libra cusp, through Libra, Scorpio and Sagittarius, resting along the Sagittarius/Capricorn cusp, ending the decade in Capricorn.

The stars and the decade

The movement of planets through the dynastic sign of Sagittarius brought doubt and uncertainty to Britain's royal family, while the planets in authoritative Capricorn brought strong government to the UK in the form of Margaret Thatcher. Ordinary people began to seriously question the *status quo* and to attempt to change it. Even in the hidden empire of China, modernization and change began to creep in. Britain went to war again by sending the gunboats to the Falkland Islands to fight off a truly old-fashioned takeover bid by the daft Argentinean dictator, General Galtieri.

Saturn is an earth planet, Neptune rules the sea, while Uranus is associated with the air. None of these planets was in their own element and this may have had something to do with the increasing number of natural and man-made disasters that disrupted the surface of the earth during this decade. The first space shuttle flight took place in 1981 and the remainder of the decade reflected many people's interest in extra-terrestrial life in the form of films and television programmes. ET went home. Black rap music and the casual use of drugs became a normal part of the youth scene. Maybe the movement of escapist Neptune through the 'outer space' sign of Sagittarius had something to do with this.

1990 – 1999

Pluto began the decade in Scorpio, moving in and out of Sagittarius until 1995 remaining there for the rest of the decade. Neptune began the decade in Capricorn, travelling back and forth over the cusp of Aquarius, ending the decade in Aquarius, Uranus moved in and out of Aquarius, remaining there from 1996 onwards. Saturn travelled from Capricorn, through Aquarius, Pisces (and back again), then on through Pisces, Aries, in and out of Taurus, finally ending the decade in Taurus.

The stars and the decade

The Aquarian emphasis has brought advances in science and technology and a time when computers are common even in the depths of darkest Africa. The logic and fairness of Aquarius does seem to have affected many of the peoples of the earth. Pluto in the open sign of Sagittarius brought much governmental secrecy to an end, it will also transform the traditional dynasties of many countries before it leaves them for good. The aftermath of the dreadful and tragic death of Princess Diana in 1997 put a rocket under the creaking 19th-century habits of British royalty.

The final decade began with yet another war – this time the Gulf War – which sent a serious signal to all those who fancy trying their hand at international bullying or the 19th-century tactics of pinching your neighbour's land and resources. Uranus's last fling in Capricorn tore up the earth with volcanoes and earthquakes, and its stay in Aquarius seems to be keeping this pattern going. Saturn in Pisces, opposite the 'health' sign of Virgo is happily bringing new killer viruses into being and encouraging old ones to build up resistance to antibiotics. The bubonic plague is alive and well in tropical countries along with plenty of other plagues that either are, or are becoming resistant to modern medicines. Oddly enough the planetary line-up in 1997 was similar to that of the time of the great plague of London in 1665!

Films, the arts, architecture all showed signs of beginning an exciting period of revolution in 1998. Life became more electronic and computer-based for the younger generation while in the old world, the vast army of the elderly began to struggle with a far less certain world of old-age poverty and strange and frightening innovations. Keeping up to date and learning to adapt is the only way to survive now, even for the old folks.

It is interesting to note that the first event of importance to shock Europe in this century was the morganatic marriage of Franz Ferdinand, the heir to the massively powerful Austro-Hungarian throne. This took place in the summer of 1900. The unpopularity of this controlling and repressive empire fell on its head in Sarajevo on the 28th of July 1914. This mighty empire is now almost forgotten, but its death throes are still being played out in and around Sarajevo today - which only goes to show how long it can take for anything to be settled.

Technically the twentieth century only ends at the beginning of the year 2001 but most of us will be celebrating the end of the century and the end of the millennium and the end of the last day of 1999 - that is if we are all here of course! A famous prediction of global disaster comes from the writings of the French writer, doctor and astrologer Nostradamus (1503–66):

- The year 1999, seventh month,
- From the sky will come a great King of Terror:
- To bring back to life the great King of the Mongols,
- Before and after Mars reigns.
  (Quatrain X:72 from the *Centuries*)

Jonathan has worked out that with the adjustments of the calendar from the time of Nostradamus, the date of the predicted disaster will be the 11th of August 1999. As it happens there will be a total eclipse of the Sun at ten past eleven on that day at 18 degrees of Leo. We have already seen how the signs of Cancer, Leo and Libra seem to be the ones that are most clearly associated with war and this reference to 'Mars reigning' is the fact that Mars is the god of war. Therefore, the prediction suggests that an Oriental king will wage a war from the sky that brings terror to the world. Some people have suggested that this event would bring about the end of the world but that is not what the prediction actually says. A look back over the 1900s has proved this whole century to be one of terror from the skies but it would be awful to think that there would be yet another war, this time emanating from Mongolia. Terrible but not altogether impossible to imagine I guess. Well, let us hope that we are all here for us to write and for you to enjoy the next set of zodiac books for the turn of the millennium and beyond.

2000 onwards: a very brief look forward

The scientific exploration and eventual colonization of space is on the way now. Scorpio rules fossil fuels and there will be no major planets passing through this sign for quite a while so alternative fuel sources will have to be sought. Maybe it will be the entry of Uranus into the pioneering sign of Aries in January 2012 that will make a start on this. The unusual line up of the 'ancient seven' planets of Sun, Moon, Mercury, Venus, Mars and Saturn in Taurus on the 5th of May 2000 will be interesting. Taurus represents such matters as land, farming, building, cooking, flowers, the sensual beauty of music, dancing and the arts. Jonathan and Sasha will work out the astrological possibilities for the future in depth and put out ideas together for you in a future book.

The Essential Leo

YOUR RULING PLANET Your ruling body is the Sun. The Sun is associated with the Roman god Apollo, who was the god of music, poetry, prophecy, reason, light and healing.

YOUR SYMBOL The lion is your symbol. It has always been associated with strong men, and it commemorates the first of the labours of Hercules, which was the defeat of the enormous Nemean lion; Samson, too, fought the lion. Typical Leos, and even more so for those who have Leo as a rising sign, actually look a bit like the king of the jungle.

PARTS OF THE BODY The spine, heart, arteries and the circulation.

YOUR GOOD BITS You are honest, decent, hard-working and a good organizer. You rarely give up or give in to despair. You are extremely generous and affectionate.

YOUR BAD BITS You can be arrogant and bad-tempered when you don't get your own way. You are also self-centred and sometimes extravagant.

YOUR WEAKNESSES You enjoy being the centre of attention and playing the boss.

YOUR BEST DAY Sunday. This is the Sun's day.

YOUR WORST DAY Saturday. Probably because this is Saturn's day, and Saturn can put a blight on anything when it wants to.

YOUR COLOURS Gold, yellow, creamy colours, orange.

CITIES Rome, Bombay, Prague, Damascus, Los Angeles, Chicago, Philadelphia.

COUNTRIES France, Italy, Romania, Czechoslovakia.

HOLIDAYS Anywhere expensive, sophisticated and luxurious. The Raffles Hotel in Singapore, or a trip on the QE2 would do nicely.

LEO

YOUR FAVOURITE CAR The flashiest possible sports car with great wheel hubs, the lightest and fastest engine and a pose value of 100 plus!

YOUR FAVOURITE MEAL OUT You enjoy the best of the best, and that includes good service, excellent presentation and spotless linen. Many Leos enjoy a buffet or a salad bar. Astrological tradition also suggests saffron and citrus fruits as Leo favourites.

YOUR FAVOURITE DRINK Most Leos can't drink much, but when you do have a drink it is likely to be spirits such as Scotch, bourbon, vodka or brandy, probably with a mixer such as tonic or dry ginger.

YOUR HERBS Camomile, saffron, rosemary.

YOUR TREES Ash, palm.

YOUR FLOWERS Marigold, nasturtium, sunflower, cyclamen.

YOUR ANIMALS Lion, starfish, crocodile, swan, peacock.

YOUR METAL Gold.

YOUR GEMS There are various gems associated with your sign, such as the diamond, zircon, ruby, sardonyx and tiger's eye.

MODE OF DRESS Rather flamboyant, colourful clothes, preferably with designer labels.

YOUR CAREERS Running a company, working with children, performing and generally doing something creative. Anything that is glamorous and charismatic.

YOUR FRIENDS You prefer the company of interesting and even outrageous people who achieve success in their own field.

YOUR ENEMIES Takers, whiners, dull and stuffy types. Those who try to upstage you.

YOUR FAVOURITE GIFT Leos love a touch of luxury and gold is your lucky metal, so gold jewellery or a gold watch would please you. Both sexes enjoy novelties and toys, so something like a quirky juke-box radio or an outdoor game would be nice. Aromatic toiletries, perfumes and aftershave are also very acceptable. You might appreciate a year's membership of an up-market sports, health or country club.

YOUR IDEAL HOME A large, luxurious home in a nice area. Your home is neither untidy nor sterile, it is comfortable with excellent quality goods and furnishings that you live with for as long as possible before replacing. However, your electrical and hi-fi equipment is usually brand new. There must be a garden or play area for your children and their friends.

YOUR FAVOURITE BOOKS You love a good read, so epic novels appeal to you. Also thrillers and whodunits.

YOUR FAVOURITE MUSIC Lively music, light classical music, dance tunes, romantic pop music.

YOUR GAMES AND SPORTS Leos are often good swimmers and you also enjoy tennis and badminton. Dancing is a favourite.

YOUR PAST AND FUTURE LIVES There are many theories about past lives and even some about future ones, but we suggest that your immediate past life was ruled by the sign previous to Leo and that your future life will be governed by the sign that follows Leo. Therefore you were Cancer in your previous life and will be Virgo in the next. If you want to know all about either of these signs, zip straight out to the shops and buy our books on them!

YOUR LUCKY NUMBER Your lucky number is 5. To find your lucky number on a raffle ticket or something similar, first add the numbers together. For example, if one of your lottery numbers is 28, add 2 + 8 to make 10; then add 1 + 0, to give the root number of 1. The number 316 on a raffle ticket works in the same way. Add 3 + 1 + 6 to make 10: then add 1 + 0, making 1. As your lucky number is any number that adds up to 5, numbers 14, 212, 95 or similar would do. A selection of lottery numbers should include some of the following: 5, 14, 23, 32 and 41.

Your Sun Sign

Your Sun Sign is determined by your date of birth.
Thus anyone born between 21st March and 20th April is Aries and so
on through the calendar. Your Rising Sign (see page 36)
is determined by the day and time of your birth.

L E O

RULED BY THE SUN
23rd July to 23rd August

Leo is a masculine, fire sign whose symbol is the lion. This adds leadership, pride and an adventurous, courageous but stubborn nature.

All Leos have high standards and you don't like to let yourselves or anyone else down. You enjoy being seen as a person of substance and status and you prefer to be in a position to help others than to have to go cap in hand to them. Your pride would not allow you to live or work in a situation which you considered beneath you. Sure, you can do some pretty menial jobs when necessary, but you are far more comfortable working in an exciting area where you can jet off to glamorous places and influence the more mundane members of planet Earth. You won't stand for being treated with contempt or being ridiculed, but you are also aware of other people's need for dignity, so you are rarely offensive or hurtful. You can become surprisingly downhearted on occasion, but you don't usually stay depressed for long and your confidence returns fairly quickly. The thing that really saves your bacon when times get hard is your joyful sense of humour.

Leo faults include impatience and a tendency to overdramatize problems. You become irritable when things go wrong and quite sarcastic when ill, under pressure or overtired. You live in the fast lane, working and playing very hard but you must remember to build in times for rest and recovery, and even periods of time away from other people in order to recharge your psychic batteries. Unlike the members of your neighbouring sign of Cancer, you don't live through others, but prefer to get out there into the hurl-burly and achieve greatness for yourself. You can, however, be a very pushy parent because you want your children to achieve as much and more than you have yourself.

You are generous and kind and you will do anything you can to help others, especially the members of your own family. You would never stand in the way of a partner who wanted to get on in life; however, you would be unhappy with one who tried to hold you back or who prevented you from getting your share of the limelight. You excel as a family member and you enjoy keeping in touch with your relatives, but you are not the type to cling. You understand that your children want to leave the nest when the time comes and you encourage them to become independent. You are a very loyal and dependable marriage partner, as long as you are sure that you are loved and that you occupy the centre place in the family hierarchy. You are unlikely to go off and have a fling out of simple curiosity, but you could do so if you felt that you were undervalued and unloved by those around you. You are one of the fixed signs which suggests that you would only break up a marriage or leave a job half-done if it became absolutely necessary. Some of you will stick to a difficult partner as long as there is some sexual chemistry remaining.

You like the best of everything and you can be the kind of snob who buys designer-label clothes and drives a flashy car. You love to travel to smart places and to holiday in five-star comfort. You can be very extravagant and indulgent with yourself and towards others. Your values are traditional, and although there are a few rogue Leos around who seem to have no standards at all, these are untypical.

All the Other Sun Signs

ARIES
21st March to 20th April

Ariens can get anything they want off the ground, but they may land back down again with a bump. Quick to think and to act, Ariens are often intelligent and have little patience with fools. This includes anyone who is slower than themselves.

They are not the tidiest of people and they are impatient with details, except when engaged upon their special subject; then Ariens can fiddle around for hours. They are willing to make huge financial sacrifices for their families and they can put up with relatives living with them as long as this leaves them free to do their own thing. Aries women are decisive and competitive at work but many are disinterested in homemaking. They might consider giving up a relationship if it interfered with their ambitions. Highly sexed and experimental, they are faithful while in love but, if love begins to fade, they start to look around. Ariens may tell themselves that they are only looking for amusement, but they may end up in a fulfilling relationship with someone else's partner. This kind of situation offers the continuity and emotional support which they need with no danger of boredom or entrapment.

Their faults are those of impatience and impetuosity, coupled with a hot temper. They can pick a furious row with a supposed adversary, tear him or her to pieces then walk away from the situation five minutes later, forgetting all about it. Unfortunately, the poor victim can't always shake off the effects of the row in quite the same way. However, Arien cheerfulness, spontaneous generosity and kindness make them the greatest friends to have.

TAURUS
21st April to 21st May

These people are practical and persevering. Taureans are solid and reliable, regular in habits, sometimes a bit wet behind the ears and stubborn as mules. Their love of money and the comfort it can bring may make them very materialistic in outlook. They are most suited to a practical career which brings with it few surprises and plenty of money. However, they have a strong artistic streak which can be expressed in work, hobbies and interests.

Some Taureans are quick and clever, highly amusing and quite outrageous in appearance, but underneath this crazy exterior is a background of true talent and very hard work. This type may be a touch arrogant. Other Taureans hate to be rushed or hassled, preferring to work quietly and thoroughly at their own pace. They take relationships very seriously and make safe and reliable partners. They may keep their worries to themselves but they are not usually liars or sexually untrustworthy.

Being so very sensual as well as patient, these people make excellent lovers. Their biggest downfall comes later in life when they have a tendency to plonk themselves down in front of the television night after night, tuning out the rest of the world. Another problem with some Taureans is their 'pet hate', which they'll harp on about at any given opportunity. Their virtues are common sense, loyalty, responsibility and a pleasant, non-hostile approach to others. Taureans are much brighter than anyone gives them credit, and it is hard to beat them in an argument because they usually know what they are talking about. If a Taurean is on your side, they make wonderful friends and comfortable and capable colleagues.

GEMINI
22nd May to 21st June

Geminis are often accused of being short on intellect and unable to stick to anyone or anything for long. In a nutshell, great fun at a party but totally unreliable. This is unfair: nobody works harder, is more reliable or capable than Geminis when they put their mind to a task, especially if there is a chance of making large sums of money! Unfortunately, they have a low boredom threshold and they can drift away from something or someone when it no longer interests them. They like to be busy, with plenty of variety in their lives and the opportunity to communicate with others. Their forte lies in the communications industry where they shamelessly pinch ideas and improve on them. Many Geminis are highly ambitious people who won't allow anything or anyone to stand in their way.

They are surprisingly constant in relationships, often marrying for life but, if it doesn't work out, they will walk out and put the experience behind them. Geminis need relationships and if one fails, they will soon start looking for the next. Faithfulness is another story, however, because the famous Gemini curiosity can lead to any number of adventures. Geminis educate their children well while neglecting to see whether they have a clean shirt. The house is full of books, videos, televisions, CDs, newspapers and magazines and there is a phone in every room as well as in the car, the loo and the Gemini lady's handbag.

CANCER
22nd June to 23rd July

Cancerians look for security on the one hand and adventure and novelty on the other. They are popular because they really listen to what others are saying. Their own voices are attractive too. They are naturals for sales work and in any kind of advisory capacity. Where their own problems are concerned, they can disappear inside themselves and brood, which makes it hard for others to understand them. Cancerians spend a good deal of time worrying about their families and, even more so, about money. They appear soft but are very hard to influence.

Many Cancerians are small traders and many more work in teaching or the caring professions. They have a feel for history, perhaps collecting historical mementoes, and their memories are excellent. They need to have a home but they love to travel away from it, being happy in the knowledge that it is there waiting for them to come back to. There are a few Cancerians who seem to drift through life and expect other members of their family to keep them.

Romantically, they prefer to be settled and they fear being alone. A marriage would need to be really bad before they consider leaving, and if they do, they soon look for a new partner. These people can be scoundrels in business because they hate parting with money once they have their hands on it. However, their charm and intelligence usually manage to get them out of trouble.

VIRGO
24th August to 23rd September

Virgos are highly intelligent, interested in everything and everyone and happy to be busy with many jobs and hobbies. Many have some kind of specialized knowledge and most are good with their hands, but their nit-picking ways can infuriate colleagues. They find it hard to discuss their innermost feelings and this can make them hard to understand. In many ways, they are happier doing something practical than dealing with relationships. Virgos can also overdo the self-sacrificial bit and make themselves martyrs to other people's impractical lifestyles. They are willing to fit in with whatever is going on and can adjust to most things, but they mustn't neglect their own needs.

Although excellent communicators and wonderfully witty conversationalists, Virgos prefer to express their deepest feelings by actions rather than words. Most avoid touching all but very close friends and family members and many find lovey-dovey behaviour embarrassing. They can be very highly sexed and may use this as a way of expressing love. Virgos are criticized a good deal as children and are often made to feel unwelcome in their childhood homes. In turn, they become very critical of others and they can use this in order to wound.

Many Virgos overcome inhibitions by taking up acting, music, cookery or sports. Acting is particularly common to this sign because it allows them to put aside their fears and take on the mantle of someone quite different. They are shy and slow to make friends but when they do accept someone, they are the loyalest, gentlest and kindest of companions. They are great company and have a wonderful sense of humour.

LIBRA
24th September to 23rd October

Librans have a deceptive appearance, looking soft but being tough and quite selfish underneath. Astrological tradition tells us that this sign is dedicated to marriage, but a high proportion of them prefer to remain single, particularly when a difficult relationship comes to an end. These people are great to tell secrets to because they never listen to anything properly and promptly forget whatever is said. The confusion between their desire to co-operate with others and the need for self-expression is even more evident when at work. The best job is one where they are a part of an organization but able to take responsibility and make their own decisions.

While some Librans are shy and lacking in confidence, others are strong and determined with definite leadership qualities. All need to find a job that entails dealing with others and which does not wear out their delicate nerves. All Librans are charming, sophisticated and diplomatic, but can be confusing for others. All have a strong sense of justice and fair play but most haven't the strength to take on a determinedly lame duck. They project an image which is attractive, chosen to represent their sense of status and refinement. Being inclined to experiment sexually, they are not the most faithful of partners and even goody-goody Librans are terrible flirts.

SCORPIO
24th October to 22nd November

Reliable, resourceful and enduring, Scorpios seem to be the strong men and women of the zodiac. But are they really? They can be nasty at times, dishing out what they see as the truth, no matter how unwelcome. Their own feelings are sensitive and they are easily hurt, but they won't show any hurt or weakness in themselves to others. When they are very low or unhappy, this turns inwards, attacking their immune systems and making them ill. However, they have great resilience and they bounce back time and again from the most awful ailments.

Nobody needs to love and be loved more than a Scorpio, but their partners must stand up to them because they will give anyone they don't respect a very hard time indeed. They are the most loyal and honest of companions, both in personal relationships and at work. One reason for this is their hatred of change or uncertainty. Scorpios enjoy being the power behind the throne with someone else occupying the hot seat. This way, they can quietly manipulate everyone, set one against another and get exactly what they want from the situation.

Scorpios' voices are their best feature, often low, well-modulated and cultured and these wonderful voices are used to the full in pleasant persuasion. These people are neither as highly sexed nor as difficult as most astrology books make out, but they do have their passions (even if these are not always for sex itself) and they like to be thought of as sexy. They love to shock and to appear slightly dangerous, but they also make kind-hearted and loyal friends, superb hosts and gentle people who are often very fond of animals. Great people when they are not being cruel, stingy or devious!

SAGITTARIUS
23rd November to 21st December

Sagittarians are great company because they are interested in everything and everyone. Broad-minded and lacking in prejudice, they are fascinated by even the strangest of people. With their optimism and humour, they are often the life and soul of the party, while they are in a good mood. They can become quite down-hearted, crabby and awkward on occasion, but not usually for long. They can be hurtful to others because they cannot resist speaking what they see as the truth, even if it causes embarrassment. However, their tactlessness is usually innocent and they have no desire to hurt.

Sagittarians need an unconventional lifestyle, preferably one which allows them to travel. They cannot be cooped up in a cramped environment and they need to meet new people and to explore a variety of ideas during their day's work. Money is not their god and they will work for a pittance if they feel inspired by the task. Their values are spiritual rather than material. Many are attracted to the spiritual side of life and may be interested in the Church, philosophy, astrology and other New Age subjects. Higher education and legal matters attract them because these subjects expand and explore intellectual boundaries. Long-lived relationships may not appeal because they need to feel free and unfettered, but they can do well with a self-sufficient and independent partner. Despite all this intellectualism and need for freedom, Sagittarians have a deep need to be cuddled and touched and they need to be supported emotionally.

CAPRICORN
22nd December to 20th January

Capricorns are patient, realistic and responsible and they take life seriously. They need security but they may find this difficult to achieve. Many live on a treadmill of work, simply to pay the bills and feed the kids. They will never shun family responsibilities, even caring for distant relatives if this becomes necessary. However, they can play the martyr while doing so. These people hate coarseness, they are easily embarrassed and they hate to annoy anyone. Capricorns believe fervently in keeping the peace in their families. This doesn't mean that they cannot stand up for themselves, indeed they know how to get their own way and they won't be bullied. They are adept at using charm to get around prickly people.

Capricorns are ambitious, hard-working, patient and status-conscious and they will work their way steadily towards the top in any organization. If they run their own businesses, they need a partner with more pizzazz to deal with sales and marketing for them while they keep an eye on the books. Their nit-picking habits can infuriate others and some have a tendency to 'know best' and not to listen. These people work at their hobbies with the same kind of dedication that they put into everything else. They are faithful and reliable in relationships and it takes a great deal to make them stray. If a relationship breaks up, they take a long time to get over it. They may marry very early or delay it until middle age when they are less shy. As an earth sign, Capricorns are highly sexed but they need to be in a relationship where they can relax and gain confidence. Their best attribute is their genuine kindness and their wonderfully dry, witty sense of humour.

AQUARIUS
21st January to 19th February

Clever, friendly, kind and humane, Aquarians are the easiest people to make friends with but probably the hardest to really know. They are often more comfortable with acquaintances than with those who are close to them. Being dutiful, they would never let a member of their family go without their basic requirements, but they can be strangely, even deliberately, blind to their underlying needs and real feelings. They are more comfortable with causes and their idealistic ideas than with the day-to-day routine of family life. Their homes may reflect this lack of interest by being rather messy, although there are other Aquarians who are almost clinically house proud.

Their opinions are formed early in life and are firmly fixed. Being patient with people, they make good teachers and are, themselves, always willing to learn something new. But are they willing to go out and earn a living? Some are, many are not. These people can be extremely eccentric in the way they dress or the way they live. They make a point of being 'different' and they can actually feel very unsettled and uneasy if made to conform, even outwardly. Their restless, sceptical minds mean that they need an alternative kind of lifestyle which stretches them mentally.

In relationships, they are surprisingly constant and faithful and they only stray when they know in their hearts that there is no longer anything to be gained from staying put. Aquarians are often very attached to the first real commitment in their lives and they can even remarry a previously divorced partner. Their sexuality fluctuates, perhaps peaking for some years then pushed aside while something else occupies their energies, then high again. Many Aquarians are extremely highly sexed and very clever and active in bed.

PISCES
20th February to 20th March

This idealistic, dreamy, kind and impractical sign needs a lot of understanding. They have a fractured personality which has so many sides and so many moods that they probably don't even understand themselves. Nobody is more kind, thoughtful and caring, but they have a tendency to drift away from people and responsibilities. When the going gets rough, they get going! Being creative, clever and resourceful, these people can achieve a great deal and really reach the top, but few of them do. Some Pisceans have a self-destruct button which they press before reaching their goal. Others do achieve success and the motivating force behind this essentially spiritual and mystical sign is often money. Many Pisceans feel insecure, most suffer some experience of poverty at some time in their early lives and they grow into adulthood determined that they will never feel that kind of uncertainty again.

Pisceans are at home in any kind of creative or caring career. Many can be found in teaching, nursing and the arts. Some find life hard and are often unhappy; many have to make tremendous sacrifices on behalf of others. This may be a pattern which repeats itself from childhood, where the message is that the Piscean's needs always come last. These people can be stubborn, awkward, selfish and quite nasty when a friendship or relationship goes sour. This is because, despite their basically kind and gentle personality, there is a side which needs to be in charge of any relationship. Pisceans make extremely faithful partners as long as the romance doesn't evaporate and their partners treat them well. Problems occur if they are mistreated or rejected, if they become bored or restless or if their alcohol intake climbs over the danger level. The Piscean lover is a sexual fantasist, so in this sphere of life anything can happen!

You and Yours

What is it like to bring up an Arien child? What kind of father does a Libran make? How does it feel to grow up with a Sagittarian mother? Whatever your own sign is, how do you appear to your parents and how do you behave towards your children?

THE LEO FATHER

These men can be wonderful fathers as long as they remember that children are not simply small and rather obstreperous adults. Leo fathers like to be involved with their children and encourage them to do well at school. They happily make sacrifices for their children and they truly want them to have the best, but they can be a bit too strict and they may demand too high a standard.

THE LEO MOTHER

Leo mothers are very caring and responsible but they cannot be satisfied with a life of pure domesticity, and need to combine motherhood with a job. These mothers don't fuss about minor details. They're prepared to put up with a certain amount of noise and disruption, but they can be irritable and they may demand too much of their children.

THE LEO CHILD

These children know almost from the day they are born that they are special. They are usually loved and wanted but they are also aware that a lot is expected from them. Leo children appear outgoing but they are surprisingly sensitive and easily hurt. They only seem to wake up to the need to study a day or so after they leave school, but they find a way to make a success of their lives.

THE ARIES FATHER

Arien men take the duties of fatherhood very seriously. They read to their children, take them on educational trips and expose them to art and music from an early age. They can push their children too hard or tyrannize the sensitive ones. The Aries father wants his children not only to have what he didn't have but also to be what he isn't. He respects those children who are high achievers and who can stand up to him.

THE ARIES MOTHER

Arien women love their children dearly and will make amazing sacrifices for them, but don't expect them to give up their jobs or their outside interests for motherhood. Competitive herself, this mother wants her children to be the best and she may push them too hard. However, she is kind-hearted, affectionate and not likely to over-discipline them. She treats her offspring as adults and is well loved in return.

THE ARIES CHILD

Arien children are hard to ignore. Lively, noisy and demanding, they try to enjoy every moment of their childhood. Despite this, they lack confidence and need reassurance. Often clever but lacking in self-discipline, they need to be made to attend school each day and to do their homework. Active and competitive, these children excel in sports, dancing or learning to play a pop music instrument.

THE TAURUS FATHER

This man cares deeply for his children and wants the best for them, but doesn't expect the impossible. He may lay the law down and he can be unsympathetic to the attitudes and interests of a new generation. He may frighten young children by shouting at them. Being a responsible parent, he offers a secure family base but he may find it hard to let them go when they want to leave.

THE TAURUS MOTHER

These women make good mothers due to their highly domesticated nature. Some are real earth mothers, baking bread and making wonderful toys and games for their children. Sane and sensible but not highly imaginative, they do best with a child who has ordinary needs and they get confused by those who are 'special' in any way. Taurus mothers are very loving but they use reasonable discipline when necessary.

THE TAURUS CHILD

Taurean children can be surprisingly demanding. Their loud voices and stubborn natures can be irritating. Plump, sturdy and strong, some are shy and retiring, while others can bully weaker children. Artistic, sensual and often musical, these children can lose themselves in creative or beautiful hobbies. They need to be encouraged to share and express love and also to avoid too many sweet foods.

THE GEMINI FATHER

Gemini fathers are fairly laid back in their approach and, while they cope well with fatherhood, they can become bored with home life and try to escape from their duties. Some are so absorbed with work that they hardly see their offspring. At home, Gemini fathers will provide books, educational toys and as much computer equipment as the child can use, and they enjoy a family game of tennis.

THE GEMINI MOTHER

These mothers can be very pushy because they see education as the road to success. They encourage a child to pursue any interest and will sacrifice time and money for this. They usually have a job outside the home and may rely on other people to do some child-minding for them. Their children cannot always count on coming home to a balanced meal, but they can talk to their mothers on any subject.

THE GEMINI CHILD

These children needs a lot of reassurance because they often feel like square pegs in round holes. They either do very well at school and incur the wrath of less able children, or they fail dismally and have to make it up later in life. They learn to read early and some have excellent mechanical ability while others excel at sports. They get bored very easily and they can be extremely irritating.

THE CANCER FATHER

A true family man who will happily embrace even stepchildren as if they were his own. Letting go of the family when they grow up is another matter. Cancerian sulks, moodiness and bouts of childishness can confuse or frighten some children, while his changeable attitude to money can make them unsure of what they should ask for. This father enjoys domesticity and child-rearing and he may be happy to swap roles.

THE CANCER MOTHER

Cancerian women are excellent home makers and cheerful and reasonable mothers, as long as they have a part-time job or an interest outside the house. They instinctively know when a child is unhappy and can deal with it in a manner which is both efficient and loving. These women have a reputation for clinging but most are quite realistic when the time comes for their brood to leave the nest.

THE CANCER CHILD

These children are shy, cautious and slow to grow up. They may achieve little at school, 'disappearing' behind louder and more demanding classmates. They can be worriers who complain about every ache and pain or suffer from imaginary fears. They may take on the mother's role in the family, dictating to their sisters and brothers at times. Gentle and loving but moody and secretive, they need a lot of love and encouragement.

THE VIRGO FATHER

These men may be embarrassed by open declarations of love and affection and find it hard to give cuddles and reassurance to small children. Yet they love their offspring dearly and will go to any lengths to see that they have the best possible education and outside activities. Virgoan men can become wrapped up in their work, forgetting to spend time relaxing and playing with their children.

THE VIRGO MOTHER

Virgoan women try hard to be good mothers because they probably had a poor childhood themselves. They love their children very much and want the best for them but they may be fussy about unnecessary details, such as dirt on the kitchen floor or the state of the children's school books. If they can keep their tensions and longings away from their children, they can be the most kindly and loving parents.

THE VIRGO CHILD

Virgoan children are practical and capable and can do very well at school, but they are not always happy. They don't always fit in and they may have difficulty making friends. They may be shy, modest and sensitive and they can find it hard to live up to their own impossibly high standards. Virgo children don't need harsh discipline, they want approval and will usually respond perfectly well to reasoned argument.

THE LIBRA FATHER

Libran men mean well, but they may not actually perform that well. They have no great desire to be fathers but welcome their children when they come along. They may slide out of the more irksome tasks by having an absorbing job or a series of equally absorbing hobbies which keep them occupied outside the home. These men do better with older children because they can talk to them.

THE LIBRA MOTHER

Libran mothers are pleasant and easy-going but some of them are more interested in their looks, their furnishings and their friends than their children. Others are very loving and kind but a bit too soft, which results in their children disrespecting them or walking all over them in later life. These mothers enjoy talking to their children and encouraging them to succeed.

THE LIBRA CHILD

These children are charming and attractive and they have no difficulty in getting on with people. They make just enough effort to get through school and only do the household jobs they cannot dodge. They may drive their parents mad with their demands for the latest gadget or gimmick. However, their common sense, sense of humour and reasonable attitude makes harsh discipline unnecessary.

THE SCORPIO FATHER

These fathers can be really awful or absolutely wonderful, and there aren't any half-measures. Good Scorpio men provide love and security because they stick closely to their homes and families and are unlikely to do a disappearing act. Difficult ones can be loud and tyrannical. These proud men want their children to be the best.

THE SCORPIO MOTHER

These mothers are either wonderful or not really maternal at all, although they try to do their best. If they take to child-rearing, they encourage their offspring educationally and in their hobbies. These mothers have no time for whiny or miserable children but they respect outgoing, talented and courageous ones, and can cope with a handful.

THE SCORPIO CHILD

Scorpio children are competitive, self-centred and unwilling to co-operate with brothers, sisters, teachers or anyone else when in an awkward mood. They can be deeply unreadable, living in a world of their own and filled with all kinds of strange angry feelings. At other times, they can be delightfully caring companions. They love animals, sports, children's organizations and group activities.

THE SAGITTARIUS FATHER

Sagittarian fathers will give their children all the education they can stand. They happily provide books, equipment and take their offspring out to see anything interesting. They may not always be available to their offspring, but they make up for it by surprising their families with tickets for sporting events or by bringing home a pet for the children. These men are cheerful and childlike themselves.

THE SAGITTARIUS MOTHER

This mother is kind, easy-going and pleasant. She may be very ordinary with suburban standards or she may be unbelievably eccentric, forcing the family to take up strange diets and filling the house with weird and wonderful people. Some opt out of child-rearing by finding childminders while others take on other people's children and a host of animals in addition to their own.

THE SAGITTARIUS CHILD

Sagittarian children love animals and the outdoor life but they are just as interested in sitting around and watching the telly as the next child. These children have plenty of friends whom they rush out and visit at every opportunity. Happy and optimistic but highly independent, they cannot be pushed in any direction. Many leave home in late their teens in order to travel.

THE CAPRICORN FATHER

These are true family men who cope with housework and child-rearing but they are sometimes too involved in work to spend much time at home. Dutiful and caring, these men are unlikely to run off with a bimbo or to leave their family wanting. However, they can be stuffy or out of touch with the younger generation. They encourage their children to do well and to behave properly.

THE CAPRICORN MOTHER

Capricorn women make good mothers but they may be inclined to fuss. Being ambitious, they want their children to do well and they teach them to respect teachers, youth leaders and so on. These mothers usually find work outside the home in order to supplement the family income. They are very loving but they can be too keen on discipline and the careful management of pocket money.

THE CAPRICORN CHILD

Capricorn children are little adults from the day they are born. They don't need much discipline or encouragement to do well at school. Modest and well behaved, they are almost too good to be true. However, they suffer badly with their nerves and can be prone to ailments such as asthma. They need to be taught to let go, have fun and enjoy their childhood. Some are too selfish or ambitious to make friends.

THE AQUARIAN FATHER

Some Aquarian men have no great desire to be fathers but they make a reasonable job of it when they have to. They cope best when their children are reasonable and intelligent but, if they are not, they tune out and ignore them. Some Aquarians will spend hours inventing games and toys for their children while all of them value education and try to push their children.

THE AQUARIAN MOTHER

Some of these mothers are too busy putting the world to rights to see what is going on in their own family. However, they are kind, reasonable and keen on education. They may be busy outside the house but they often take their children along with them. They are not fussy homemakers, and are happy to have all the neighbourhood kids in the house. They respect a child's dignity.

THE AQUARIAN CHILD

These children may be demanding when very young but they become much more reasonable when at school. They are easily bored and need outside interests. They have many friends and may spend more time in other people's homes than in their own. Very stubborn and determined, they make it quite clear from an early age that they intend to do things their own way. These children suffer from nerves.

THE PISCES FATHER

Piscean men fall into one of two categories. Some are kind and gentle, happy to take their children on outings and to introduce them to art, culture, music or sport. Others are disorganized and unpredictable. The kindly fathers don't always push their children. They encourage their kids to have friends and a pet or two.

THE PISCES MOTHER

Piscean mothers may be lax and absent-minded but they love their children and are usually loved in return. Many are too disorganized to run a perfect household so meals, laundry, etc. can be hit and miss, but their children prosper despite this, although many learn to reverse the mother/child roles. These mothers teach their offspring to appreciate animals and the environment.

THE PISCES CHILD

These sensitive children may find life difficult and they can get lost among stronger, more demanding brothers and sisters. They may drive their parents batty with their dreamy attitude and they can make a fuss over nothing. They need a secure and loving home with parents who shield them from harsh reality while encouraging them to develop their imaginative and psychic abilities.

Your Rising Sign

WHAT IS A RISING SIGN?

Your rising sign is the sign of the zodiac which was climbing up over the eastern horizon the moment you were born. This is not the same as your Sun sign; your Sun sign depends upon your date of birth, but your rising sign depends upon the time of day that you were born, combined with your date and place of birth.

The rising sign modifies your Sun sign character quite considerably, so when you have worked out which is your rising sign, read pages 39–40 to see how it modifies your Sun sign. Then take a deeper look by going back to 'All the Other Sun Signs' on page 21 and read the relevant Sun sign material there to discover more about your ascendant (rising sign) nature.

One final point is that the sign that is opposite your rising sign (or 'ascendant') is known as your 'descendant'. This shows what you want from other people, and it may give a clue as to your choice of friends, colleagues and lovers (see pages 41–3). So once you have found your rising sign and read the character interpretation, check out the character reading for your descendant to see what you are looking for in others.

How to Begin

Read through this section while following the example below. Even if you only have a vague idea of your birth time, you won't find this method difficult; just go for a rough time of birth and then read the Sun sign information for that sign to see if it fits your personality. If you seem to be more like the sign that comes before or after it, then it is likely that you were born a little earlier or later than your assumed time of birth. Don't forget to deduct an hour for summertime births.

1. Look at the illustration top right. You will notice that it has the time of day arranged around the outer circle. It looks a bit like a clock face, but it is different because it shows the whole 24-hour day in two-hour blocks.

2. Write the astrological symbol that represents the Sun (a circle with a dot in the middle) in the segment that corresponds to your time of birth. (If you were born during Daylight Saving or British Summer Time, deduct one hour from your birth time.) Our example shows someone who was born between 2 a.m. and 4 a.m.

3. Now write the name of your sign or the symbol for your sign on the line which is at the end of the block of time that your Sun falls into. Our example shows a person who was born between 2 a.m. and 4 a.m. under the sign of Pisces.

4. Either write in the names of the zodiac signs or use the symbols in their correct order (see the key below) around the chart in an anti-clockwise direction, starting from the line which is at the start of the block of time that your sun falls into.

5. The sign that appears on the left-hand side of the wheel at the 'Dawn' line is your rising sign, or ascendant. The example shows a person born with the Sun in Pisces and with Aquarius rising. Incidentally, the example chart also shows Leo, which falls on the 'Dusk' line, in the descendant. You will always find the ascendant sign on the 'Dawn' line and the descendant sign on the 'Dusk' line.

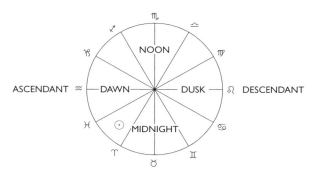

♈	Aries	♋	Cancer	♎	Libra	♑	Capricorn
♉	Taurus	♌	Leo	♏	Scorpio	♒	Aquarius
♊	Gemini	♍	Virgo	♐	Sagittarius	♓	Pisces

LEO

Here is another example for you to run through, just to make sure that you have grasped the idea correctly. This example is for a more awkward time of birth, being exactly on the line between two different blocks of time. This example is for a person with a Capricorn Sun sign who was born at 10 a.m.

1. The Sun is placed exactly on the 10 a.m. line.

2. The sign of Capricorn is placed on the 10 a.m. line.

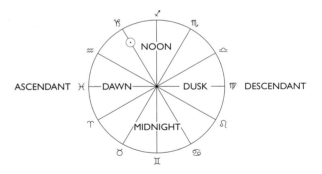

3. All the other signs are placed in astrological order (anti-clockwise) around the chart.

4. This person has the Sun in Capricorn and Pisces rising, and therefore with Virgo on the descendant.

LEO

Using the Rising Sign Finder

Please bear in mind that this method is approximate. If you want to be really sure of your rising sign, you should contact an astrologer. However, this system will work with reasonable accuracy wherever you were born. Check out the Sun and ascendant combination in the following pages. Once you've done so, if you're not quite sure you've got it right, you should also read the Sun sign character readings on pages 21–8 for the signs both before and after the rising sign you think is yours. Rising signs are such an obvious part of one's personality that one quick glance will show you which one belongs to you.

Can Your Rising Sign Tell You More about Your Future?

When it comes to tracking events, the rising sign is equal in importance to the Sun sign. So, if you want a more accurate forecast when reading newspapers or magazines, you should read the horoscope for your rising sign as well as your Sun sign. In the case of books such as this, you should really treat yourself to two: one to correspond with your rising sign, and another for your usual Sun sign, and read both each day!

How Your Rising Sign Modifies Your Sun Sign

LEO WITH ARIES RISING This fiery combination brings a childlike innocence to a courageous personality. You could be a great leader, an idealist, and also a happy family person with a nice home.

LEO WITH TAURUS RISING You have a stubborn and determined personality, and when you put your mind to it, you can accomplish a good deal. Family life is very important to you.

LEO WITH GEMINI RISING This sparkling combination makes for a sharp wit but also a kind heart. You could use your creative imagination to make music, write stories or entertain children.

LEO WITH CANCER RISING You love family life and may be very attached to your parents. Your phobias and feelings are well hidden.

LEO

LEO WITH LEO RISING This is Leo in its purest form, so what people see is what they get. You are courageous but not always as confident as you look, especially if you were born after dawn. You would be more outgoing if born before dawn.

LEO WITH VIRGO RISING Your nature is two-sided; part of you is light-hearted, and the other is deeply serious. You may be keen on New Age matters or work in the media.

LEO WITH LIBRA RISING This combination makes for a relaxed and rather lazy personality. You could be happy to let your charm and good looks do your work for you most of the time.

LEO WITH SCORPIO RISING This intense combination makes for a strong and determined personality who wants to get to the top. You may look like a career person but you need plenty of love and affection too.

LEO WITH SAGITTARIUS RISING You are quick to think and to act. You enjoy travel and you may choose to work in the tourist industry. You need personal freedom but also love and affection.

LEO WITH CAPRICORN RISING This powerful combination makes for a very hard worker. Your feelings are deep and you care passionately about your beliefs, and about those you love.

LEO WITH AQUARIUS RISING You may be very wrapped up in work or in causes. You have a strong and stubborn personality, but you do have a great sense of humour and plenty of love in your life.

LEO WITH PISCES RISING This combination could take you into the medical field or to care for others. You are split between a desire to sacrifice yourself for others and to live life for yourself.

LEO

Leo in Love

YOU NEED:

AFFECTION You need to laugh and play in the way that children and young animals do but you also need love and affection in the sexual sense. You don't appreciate a lover who only shows affection when he or she wants sex.

ENCOURAGEMENT Despite your confident exterior, you often feel unsure of yourself. If you have a loving and encouraging partner, you can achieve almost anything, but a critical one will make you thoroughly miserable.

GENEROSITY Whether we are talking about money, practical help in the home or a kind word, you need a partner who has all of these on offer at all times. The chances are that you won't rush out and spend all your lover's money, but you need to feel that if you want help, it's available.

YOU GIVE:

STEADFASTNESS You are unlikely to walk out on a partner unless a situation becomes intolerable. You are one hundred per cent behind your lover's enterprises but you have the sense not to interfere in them.

HUMOUR You love a good laugh and you have a great sense of the ridiculous. Your sunny nature means that you are rarely depressed or unhappy for long and you can cheer up a miserable lover quite quickly.

WHAT YOU CAN EXPECT FROM THE OTHER ZODIAC SIGNS:

ARIES *Truth, honesty, playfulness.* You can expect an open and honest relationship with no hidden agendas. Your Arien lover will be a bit childish at times, however.

TAURUS *Security, stability, comfort.* Taureans will stand by you and try to improve your financial position. They will create beautiful homes and gardens for their partners.

GEMINI *Stimulation, encouragement, variety.* Gemini lovers never boring; they give encouragement and are always ready for an outing. They give emotional support too.

CANCER *Emotional security, companionship, help.* Cancerians will never leave you stranded at a party or alone when suffering from the flu. They always lend a hand when asked.

LEO *Affection, fun, loyalty.* Leo lovers are very steadfast and they would avenge anyone who hurt one of their family. They enjoy romping and playing affectionate love games.

VIRGO *Clear-thinking, kindness, humour.* Virgoans make intelligent and amusing partners. They can be critical but are never unkind. They take their responsibility towards you seriously.

LIBRA *Fair-play, sensuality, advice.* Librans will listen to your problems and give balanced and sensible advice. They are wonderfully inventive, and are affectionate lovers too.

SCORPIO *Truth, passion, loyalty.* Scorpios will take your interests as seriously as they do their own. They will stick by you when the going gets tough and they wont flannel you.

SAGITTARIUS *Honesty, fun, novelty.* Theses lovers will never bore you and they'll keep up with whatever pace you set. They seek the truth and they don't keep their feelings hidden.

CAPRICORN *Companionship, common sense, laughter.* Capricorns enjoy doing things together and they won't leave you in the lurch when the going gets tough. They can make you laugh too.

AQUARIUS *Stimulation, friendship, sexuality.* Aquarians are friends as well as lovers. They are great fun because you never know what they are going to do next, in or out of bed.

PISCES *Sympathy, support, love.* These romantic lovers never let you down. They can take you with them into their personal fantasy world and they are always ready for a laugh.

WHICH SIGN ARE YOU COMPATIBLE WITH?

LEO/ARIES
Too competitive for comfort and Aries tries to dominate Leo.

LEO/LEO
As always with same sign, either great or awful.

LEO/TAURUS
Can work in some cases but Taurus could irritate Leo.

LEO/VIRGO
Can work well but Virgo a little cool for Leo.

LEO/GEMINI
Quite a nice combination as long as neither is too restless.

LEO/LIBRA
Tremendous sexual attraction but also a fight for supremacy.

LEO/CANCER
Can work well, both are interested in home and family life.

LEO/SCORPIO
Oddly enough, this match is often very successful.

LEO/SAGITTARIUS
Can work but both want the limelight and Saggy can irritate Leo.

LEO/CAPRICORN
Leo inspires Capricorn who, in turn, steadies and encourages Leo.

LEO/AQUARIUS
Either very successful or very difficult, due to joint obstinacy.

LEO/PISCES
Both are creative and attracted to show-biz and glamour so OK.

Your Prospects for 1999

LOVE

With both Uranus and Neptune in the area of your chart devoted to settled relationships and four eclipses involving you and your relationships with others, this is clearly not going to be an easy year. There may be some very good moments when things go very well and where there is more fun and excitement than usual, but this will be offset by some real difficulties at other times. The best times will be during the first half of the year while the main problems will arise late in July and August and it will take until about November to finally sort them out. You may decide to part from an association that is no longer viable and you could equally well fall suddenly and deeply in love with someone new. The problem is that you may not be able to see things as clearly as you should and you could invest a partner with all kinds of qualities that they simply couldn't be expected to have. If you do this, you will end up being disappointed. It is equally possible that your thinking is perfectly clear but that your lover misinforms you about his or her intentions. If you do find yourself in any kind of confusing off-and-on romance, things will become clearer during the second half of the year. By the end of the year, you will be less likely to have the wool pulled over your eyes, even if it is you yourself that has been doing the wool pulling.

MONEY AND WORK

Much of the confusion that has surrounded your working life over the past few years will now clear away. Your job may not be as exciting as it has been in former years but it will settle down into a workable routine. However, in January there will be a good deal of communication to do with work, and if you are looking for a new job, this would be a good time to do so. You will be particularly busy and successful during October and November. The series of eclipses that I mentioned earlier will have effects on many areas of your life and these could upset some of your work or financial plans during January, February and again in August and September. However, these do clear the air, allowing a new approach and if necessary a new start. Financially speaking, there may be a short, sharp setback in August, possibly due to overspending or too many purchases at the same time. Otherwise, this should be a better year financially and money could come from unexpected outside sources right at the start of the year. Oddly enough, this is one of those years where gambling and speculating could bring success, so if you like to make the odd wager this is the year in which to try your luck.

HEALTH

Your health should be good this year and your energy level will improve as the year progresses. However, you must guard against injury to your hands, wrists, arms and shoulders during July. Bladder infections or a reaction to something like sugary or fatty foods are possible during August and September. Despite these admittedly slight possibilities, this should be a healthy year for you.

FAMILY AND HOME

Your home, family and domestic circumstances are likely to be a very unsettled area of your life this year. Mars will bring upheavals during the first part of the year and Mercury will stir the pot during October and November. This could bring a move of house and a changes in the family line-up. Therefore, there may be additions to the family while others move on to make part of their lives outside of your family home. Elderly parents or grandparents may go through difficult times and you could find yourself running backwards and forwards between those who need you.

LUCK

An overseas trip would be a lucky break for you this year and you may be able to get a real holiday bargain. Gambling and speculating will be better starred for you than is usual now, so it might be worth trying a few small wagers here and there. However, it might be better to avoid this during the first couple of months of the year when your luck will not be at its best.

LEO

The Aspects and their Astrological Meanings

CONJUNCT   This shows important events which are usually, but not always, good.

SEXTILE   Good, particularly for work and mental activity.

SQUARE   Difficult, challenging.

TRINE   Great for romance, family life and creativity.

OPPOSITE   Awkward, depressing, challenging.

INTO   This shows when a particular planet enters a new sign of the zodiac, thus setting off a new phase or a new set of circumstances.

DIRECT   When a planet resumes normal direct motion.

RETROGRADE When a planet apparently begins to go backwards.

VOID   When the Moon makes no aspect to any planet.

September at a Glance

LOVE	❤	❤	❤		
WORK	★	★	★	★	★
MONEY	£	£	£	£	£
HEALTH	✚	✚			
LUCK	☡	☡	☡		

TUESDAY, 1ST SEPTEMBER
Moon trine Saturn

If you are looking for a new job or seeking recognition or promotion in an existing one, today should fulfil your hopes. The Lunar aspect to Saturn shows that you will receive a reward from on high.

WEDNESDAY, 2ND SEPTEMBER
Void Moon

The term 'void of course' means that neither the Moon nor any of the other planets is making any important aspects during the course of their travels today. When this kind of day occurs, the worst thing you can do is try to start something new or get anything important off the ground. Stick to routine tasks!

THURSDAY, 3RD SEPTEMBER
Moon conjunct Neptune

Wrap up warm and take care of your delicate chest, because the conjunction of the Moon and Neptune could makes you prone to coughs and sneezes today. Take care too when working at home or in the office, because your mind won't be on the job!

FRIDAY, 4TH SEPTEMBER
Mars opposite Uranus

Something, and maybe more than one thing, will go inexplicably wrong today. You may do or say something just to be polite, only to be put firmly in your place and made to feel like a nonentity. Don't let it get you down.

SATURDAY, 5TH SEPTEMBER
Moon opposite Venus

The Moon opposes Venus today and this reveals a deeply compassionate side of your nature. If you're involved in a permanent partnership, it's important to pay extra attention to the love of your life. It's too easy to give the impression that you're cold and aloof just now simply because you feel vulnerable. It's not really your fault, but as long as you're aware of the danger you can do something about it. Remember that a single gesture of affection is worth a thousand words.

SUNDAY, 6TH SEPTEMBER
Full Moon eclipse

Today's Full Moon should add a touch of spice to your intimate life. Sexually you're a dynamo, with more libido than you know what to do with! In financial affairs this lunation will accent wise investments and insurance affairs. Look to the future now, although the present has a lot going for it, too.

MONDAY, 7TH SEPTEMBER
Moon sextile Neptune

Discard your hang-ups and be prepared to react in a wild and wanton manner to a sexual proposition that comes your way. Do yourself a favour and give in to temptation!

TUESDAY, 8TH SEPTEMBER
Mercury into Virgo

Mercury's entry into your Solar house of possessions and finances turns your attention to economic realities. If you've overspent for some reason, then the next few weeks should help you sort out a practical financial strategy to put your savings back on an even keel. The keen insight that Mercury provides shows that this is a good opportunity to add to your cash resources.

WEDNESDAY, 9TH SEPTEMBER
Mercury trine Saturn

There's very little in the professional sphere that's beyond you at the moment. When it comes to deep thought and swift perception, you're a master! Others will turn to you for wise advice and you'll be able to oblige them.

THURSDAY, 10TH SEPTEMBER
Venus trine Saturn

Aside from being the planet of love, Venus also is an indicator of financial well-being. Today's aspect between Venus and Saturn allows you to put your cash affairs in order. You will be thrifty and sensible, and able to amass your resources for the future.

FRIDAY, 11TH SEPTEMBER
Mercury conjunct Venus

There's nothing that pleases you more than a stimulating conversation with people you feel in tune with – in luxurious surroundings! And, if you've got any sense of purpose, that's exactly what you'll arrange for today. You could pick up some financial tips, too.

SATURDAY, 12TH SEPTEMBER
Moon sextile Mars

A friend may drop in just when you are struggling to do something tiresome and complicated. This will prove to be a blessing in disguise, because they'll give a helping hand.

SUNDAY, 13TH SEPTEMBER
Moon square Jupiter

Your lover could show a sudden flash of jealousy or irritation about your relationship with your friends. If this is simply a one-off problem, then don't worry about it; we all get irked by our partner's friends or family from time to time. However, if this is part of a campaign to isolate you from other people, you will need to examine your partner's motives to work out what it all means.

MONDAY, 14TH SEPTEMBER
Moon sextile Venus

It would be a marvellous idea to get away from the rat race today. The Lunar aspect to Venus shows that your mind isn't on worldly duties at all, so relax that fevered brow and restore your energies by taking it easy. It doesn't matter what you do to pass the time, as long as you enjoy yourself. Perhaps you should indulge in a little luxury – the treat will do you good.

TUESDAY, 15TH SEPTEMBER
Moon sextile Sun

A final rethink before you splash out on something expensive will reveal that you've forgotten about an important item. Don't worry though, you've still got time to make that final purchase. You could also receive a surprise gift.

LEO

WEDNESDAY, 16TH SEPTEMBER
Sun opposite Jupiter

This could turn out to be an expensive day and, worse still, you and your partner could manage to waste your own and each other's money. Don't fight about it because everyone gets days like this sometimes, and they are balanced by the occasional windfall that comes our way. You may pay a karmic debt today – what goes around, comes around.

THURSDAY, 17TH SEPTEMBER
Moon conjunct Mars

Today's aspect could give you a head-rush! Well, it certainly will if you try standing on your head – and that's just one of the crazy things you might do! Your emotions will be close to the surface and you may feel angry or just generally anxious. Although there appears to be no obvious reason for this, the cause is a combination of many things that have been building up over the last few weeks.

FRIDAY, 18TH SEPTEMBER
Moon trine Saturn

An older friend could come up with a stunning financial suggestion today. Give it the thought it deserves and you'll find that with just a little effort you can improve your cash situation.

SATURDAY, 19TH SEPTEMBER
Mercury opposite Jupiter

Other people will be extremely helpful or a complete pain in the neck (or a bit of both) at the moment. You may also have more than the usual amount of legal, official or insurance matters to deal with soon.

SUNDAY, 20TH SEPTEMBER
New Moon

The New Moon in your house of finance and possessions encourages you to re-evaluate everything that you regard as important. You may find that you've been basing your ideas of success on envy of others and judging your own accomplishments by materialism alone. Perhaps you've already achieved a level of security and are now looking for another challenge? Your future economic fortunes depend on your actions now. Perhaps a visit to a bank manager or financial expert would be a good idea to get your ideas into perspective. Improvements in your finances are not only possible but likely over the next few weeks.

LEO

MONDAY, 21ST SEPTEMBER
Moon sextile Pluto

There should be some wonderful news on the way to you today. This may be about a business deal or it may concern your spouse or partner. Money and joint ventures seem to be well starred just now, and creative projects should really go with a bang.

TUESDAY, 22ND SEPTEMBER
Sun trine Neptune

The love of money may be the root of all evil, but we cannot do without it altogether – and we all love to be on the receiving end of a windfall! You should be the winner in the financial stakes today, if only in a strange, offbeat way.

WEDNESDAY, 23RD SEPTEMBER
Sun into Libra

This is the start of a rather busy period in which you will be dealing with correspondence, getting on the telephone and rushing around your neighbourhood at top speed. For the next month or so your days will be filled with activity and you will be buzzing from one job to another like a demented bee. Enjoy the success and the achievement that this brings, but do remember to relax a little from time to time.

THURSDAY, 24TH SEPTEMBER
Mercury into Libra

Mercury enters your Solar house of communications, travel and education from today, so this is the start of a period of chat, information and gossip. Close friends and neighbours may have serious concerns about the environment that you'd be wise to listen to. Of course you have a few salient points to add yourself, so don't be afraid to make your views known. Anything connected to journeys and schooling should go well now.

FRIDAY, 25TH SEPTEMBER
Sun conjunct Mercury

You could be struck by a really good idea today and, if so, discuss it with others to clarify your mind on one or two points. There could be good news in connection with other family members, especially sisters and brothers. Neighbours could also give you a helping hand.

LEO

SATURDAY, 26TH SEPTEMBER
Moon conjunct Pluto

You seem to be in a very strong position now and it is worth reminding you not to use this against others by throwing your weight around. You may actually be able to do one or two things more quickly, easily or efficiently than others now, but your efforts will be better appreciated if you use a little tact. If your emotions are running high, try making love to someone, rather than war!

SUNDAY, 27TH SEPTEMBER
Mercury sextile Pluto

If you take a look around your neighbourhood today, you'll be sure to locate a bargain or two. You may have to negotiate for what you want, but that's all part of the fun, isn't it?

MONDAY, 28TH SEPTEMBER
Moon trine Saturn

You should be in a businesslike mood today. The pressure's on and there'll be little opportunity for frivolity. At least all this hard work will pay off, because you'll be determined to enjoy the fruits of your labour.

TUESDAY, 29TH SEPTEMBER
Sun sextile Pluto

Don't let other people obscure the picture today. If there's something you have to say or find out, particularly in relation to affairs of the heart, make sure that you're crystal clear in all you say.

WEDNESDAY, 30TH SEPTEMBER
Venus into Libra

The entry of Venus into your Solar house of communication adds charm and an ability to win your own way by persuasion alone. Someone will find your opinions very attractive, so a more than passing interest will be awakened by a casual conversation. Short journeys will also be fortunate, leading to much needed (and quite painless) life lessons.

October at a Glance

LOVE	❤	❤	❤		
WORK	★	★	★		
MONEY	£	£	£	£	£
HEALTH	✚				
LUCK	♘	♘	♘	♘	

THURSDAY, 1ST OCTOBER
Sun trine Uranus

You and your partner are facing changes at the moment, but there is no reason for trepidation because the outcome will be positive. There may be more communication with your family than usual and friends will also drop in, bringing interesting and exciting news of their own.

FRIDAY, 2ND OCTOBER
Moon opposite Mars

You can be your own worst enemy sometimes, especially when impatience descends into total chaos. The fact that you've only got yourself to blame just makes things worse, because you aren't in the most reasonable mood when the Moon opposes Mars. If you're wise, don't be rushed in anything today. You'll only have to start again at square one, and if that happens you're likely to take your frustration out on your long-suffering partner.

SATURDAY, 3RD OCTOBER
Moon square Pluto

You're in a passionate frame of mind and your thoughts will stray back to memories of intimate moments again and again. You'll also be busy thinking about how to make your sensual fantasies come true! If by chance your attention is diverted to the real world, you'll find that a youngster is in a particularly awkward and obstructive mood.

SUNDAY, 4TH OCTOBER
Moon conjunct Jupiter

It's a fortunate day for money matters, and many of you could receive a small windfall – not enough to retire on, but sufficient to prompt a celebration. A pleasure-loving mood takes a hold and you'll do nothing to avoid it.

MONDAY, 5TH OCTOBER
Venus sextile Pluto

The artistically inclined will do very well out of today's aspect between Venus and Pluto. Inspiration strikes with force, and you'll make an ingenious contribution to the work or domestic scene. For those of a romantic temperament, a secret assignation is forecast.

TUESDAY, 6TH OCTOBER
Full Moon

Today's Full Moon concentrates on your higher mind and gives a culturally expansive perspective to your thinking. Anything connected with new learning, higher education and foreign affairs is well starred for the next month. Your intellect will be on top form and you'll have little patience with anything that restricts your movements. You need to flex your mental muscles!

WEDNESDAY, 7TH OCTOBER
Mars into Virgo

The energetic potential of Mars will help your finances from today. Personal wealth is bound to be increased while this most energetic of planets remains in your horoscopic area of cash resources. Action speaks louder than words now, so put into effect all those plans that you've been nurturing. Swift and sure financial decisions will pay dividends in the long run.

THURSDAY, 8TH OCTOBER
Moon sextile Jupiter

This is a fortunate day on which you can sort out the most perplexing worry with ease. The optimism of Jupiter mingles with an intuitive sense of rightness in all work, health and financial dealings. In more intimate matters this aspect works to bring you and a partner closer together, while relieving both of you of the pressure of past differences.

FRIDAY, 9TH OCTOBER
Moon trine Uranus

This is an excellent day for a party. If you haven't got an excuse, then make one up because you're in the mood for fun. The more the merrier is your motto now, so invite some friends around for a gathering in your home. Single people may find a soulmate at this time.

LEO

SATURDAY, 10TH OCTOBER
Mars trine Saturn

A long-term project is drawing to a close and all it needs is one more burst of energy to bring it to a successful conclusion. It's certain that you will receive ample praise from bosses and that you'll be reimbursed for all your efforts.

SUNDAY, 11TH OCTOBER
Neptune direct

Things start to fall into place in the career sector from today. If you're asked to be of service, comply immediately; an act of kindness will stand you in good stead for the future and win the gratitude of employers. Something you do for no reward will eventually be repaid in another way. This could help your promotion prospects because you'll show what a good-hearted soul you are. Healthwise too, you'll be feeling more like your old self.

MONDAY, 12TH OCTOBER
Mercury into Scorpio

Your life is going to be extremely busy for a while now and there will be little time to sit around and rest. You will have more to do with friends, relatives, colleagues and neighbours than is usual and you could spend quite a bit of time resolving minor domestic and work problems with workmen and women of various kinds. You may also spend time and money sorting out a vehicle.

TUESDAY, 13TH OCTOBER
Moon square Mercury

You may find yourself out of sympathy with most of your family today – sisters and brothers could be a pain in the neck, and your children could drive you crazy. The problem seems to be a lack of communication, suggesting that misunderstandings will abound. Try not to get too worked up, as this phase will pass and normality will return.

WEDNESDAY, 14TH OCTOBER
Mercury sextile Mars

It's a good day to gather your family or house-mates together for a serious chat about practicalities. Clear the air and make it absolutely clear what you expect of them in the future.

THURSDAY, 15TH OCTOBER
Moon trine Saturn

The hard taskmaster Saturn is to blame for all the effort you have to put in today, but at least there's the promise of a well-earned financial reward at the end of it.

FRIDAY, 16TH OCTOBER
Moon square Pluto

Keep calm! An affair of the heart may not be going too well at the moment, yet that's no excuse to blow your top and cause a scene. Your vanity may be offended by something innocuous. Jealousy, too, is to be guarded against.

SATURDAY, 17TH OCTOBER
Mercury square Uranus

Disturbing news could come like a bolt from the blue today. Perhaps an old skeleton is rattling in the closet, or a relative makes a revelation that shakes you. The important thing is not to over-react. Whatever it is, it's not the end of the world.

SUNDAY, 18TH OCTOBER
Uranus direct

Today that distant and eccentric planet, Uranus, turns to direct motion in the relationship area of your chart. This will make it much easier for you to deal with others, and if you have been experiencing difficulties in a partnership then this will ease. There will be noticeable improvements in working relationships with colleagues now, too. Even open enemies will be easier to deal with because you'll see where they are coming from and how they intend to attack!

MONDAY, 19TH OCTOBER
Mars square Pluto

Today is fraught with problems which are brought to a head by the negative aspect between Mars and Pluto. The issues involve money and pleasure: the belt has to be tightened, and you know it. Of course, just because this is a necessity doesn't mean you won't resent it. The trouble really starts when you begin to take your irritations out on loved ones. Try to restrain your impatience, because this imposed thrift won't last forever. Although we're not suggesting you're dishonest, there is a planetary warning than anything illegal or underhand will cost you dear.

TUESDAY, 20TH OCTOBER
New Moon

The New Moon shows a change in your way of thinking and in many ways you'll know that it's time to move on. Perhaps you'll find yourself in new company, in a new home or among new friends in the near future. Your opinions are likely to change as you become influenced by more stimulating people. Perhaps you'll consider taking up an educational course of some kind.

WEDNESDAY, 21ST OCTOBER
Moon square Uranus

This is not a brilliant day for travelling. You will find all your plans become muddled and you may be delayed for several hours at an airport or railway station. If you have drive long distances, do remember to service your car before you leave home.

THURSDAY, 22ND OCTOBER
Sun square Neptune

All you want to do is sit and dream, but time, tide, people and life itself won't allow you to. You may feel like behaving in a completely irresponsible manner, but get the chores done first and then get out your paints or spend an hour or two tinkling on the piano. When all is quiet and tranquil, reminisce on old photos, enjoy a good novel or just dream an hour or two away.

FRIDAY, 23RD OCTOBER
Sun into Scorpio

The Sun moves into your Solar area of family and domestic issues for the next four weeks. These spheres of life will now achieve maximum importance. If you have neglected your home or failed to pay the right amount of attention to your family, this is the time to put things right.

SATURDAY, 24TH OCTOBER
Venus into Scorpio

This is a good time to spend in and around your home. You may want to get the garden into shape or possibly do some kind of farming work on your land. The atmosphere around you should be harmonious and happy, and you'll be pleased with your achievements. If you have been at odds with any of your relatives, then kiss and make up today.

SUNDAY, 25TH OCTOBER
Saturn into Taurus retrograde

Any movement of Saturn is bound to affect you deeply, so when the ringed orb decides to move backwards you may feel as though you are doing nothing but treading water. You could be the victim of emotional blackmail today.

LEO

MONDAY, 26TH OCTOBER
Sun conjunct Venus

There is great news for those who are dealing with property or premises now. You may discover your dream home, or you may find just the space you need to run a small business. You could get something fixed, altered or mended in the home and, if so, you will be very happy with the results. Love could come winging your way now too.

TUESDAY, 27TH OCTOBER
Moon sextile Mercury

You are full of creative ideas today and fortunately you have the energy to put them into action. You will get all the help you need from friends and neighbours if you care to ask them.

WEDNESDAY, 28TH OCTOBER
Moon square Sun

The path of true love never did run smoothly and today there seem to be a few spanners in the works. Perhaps your mood is romantic, while your partner's is purely practical.

THURSDAY, 29TH OCTOBER
Saturn square Neptune

A moody and an irascible day for you, we're afraid. Saturn and Neptune are at odds, bringing insecurities to the surface. The career picture is the main area of concern, but there may be worrying undercurrents in a close relationship too. Steady as you go!

FRIDAY, 30TH OCTOBER
Moon sextile Saturn

Practicality rears its ugly head today, but this won't dismay you. Financial affairs need careful attention now and it won't do to overlook a single detail of income and expenditure. Although money matters will worry you slightly, there's very little need for concern. Any problem highlighted now will be a temporary cash-flow glitch, not a major crisis.

SATURDAY, 31ST OCTOBER
Moon conjunct Jupiter

What a romantic day this is likely to be! The Lunar conjunction with Jupiter shows that your affections are readily given, and there will be an equal expression of love coming back to you. This is a time for togetherness and sharing.

November at a Glance

LOVE	❤		❤		❤		❤	
WORK	★							
MONEY	£		£		£		£		£
HEALTH	✚		✚		✚		✚	
LUCK	♘							

SUNDAY, 1ST NOVEMBER
Mercury into Sagittarius

Over the next two or three weeks something will capture your attention and keep you amused. You may take an interest in intellectual games such as bridge, chess or other board games, or stimulate the grey matter with quizzes or crosswords. There is a fair chance that you could win something through entering a competition of some kind. Read ahead to find the best days for lucky chances.

MONDAY, 2ND NOVEMBER
Void Moon

There are no important planetary aspects today and even the Moon is unaspected. This kind of a day is called a 'void of course Moon' day, because the Moon is void of aspects during this part of its course. The best way to approach such a day is to do what is normal and natural without starting anything new or particularly special.

TUESDAY, 3RD NOVEMBER
Moon square Neptune

A social evening could be ruined if you don't look after your digestion. We know you like exotic food, but do you think that you're asking too much of your constitution? Take it easy and say no to extra helpings. Self-denial won't go amiss!

WEDNESDAY, 4TH NOVEMBER
Full Moon

The career-orientated Full Moon urges you to reassess your aims and ambitions today. You've achieved many of the things you set out to do so many years ago, but you may not have noticed. It's time you opened your eyes to new possibilities occurring in the working environment. Perhaps you've got as far as you can on one particular path and long for a change.

THURSDAY, 5TH NOVEMBER
Moon trine Neptune

A boss or other authority figure could drop a subtle hint today. It's now becoming clear that big things are planned for you, and all you have to do is play along. Co-operation with employers is your best course now.

FRIDAY, 6TH NOVEMBER
Mercury conjunct Pluto

Your powers of observation are very strong which is a very good thing, since you're bound to have an argument or two along the way today. You can make your opponent's arguments rebound and achieve considerable influence over others.

SATURDAY, 7TH NOVEMBER
Mars opposite Jupiter

Fools rush in where angels fear to tread, and that's exactly what could happen to you if you follow your impulses today. In all money matters caution should be your watchword. Take care that you don't bite off more than you can chew with loans, mortgages and overdrafts.

SUNDAY, 8TH NOVEMBER
Venus trine Jupiter

You seem to be making some really far-reaching decisions, but you won't have to cope with this alone because your loved ones will help and support you in all you are trying to achieve. If you are in the early stages of forming a loving partnership, this could be the time to make a home and lay the foundations of your future life together.

MONDAY, 9TH NOVEMBER
Venus sextile Mars

You will probably want to do something to improve your surroundings today, so take a look around the shops to see if there are any bargains on offer. This is a good day to entertain visitors or simply to cook something special for your family. There will be good news about money coming in now and, in addition, friends of both sexes could be helpful to you and yours.

LEO

TUESDAY, 10TH NOVEMBER
Sun trine Jupiter

The Solar aspect to Jupiter shows that you are feeling more secure, both financially and in terms of family affection. Obviously the two are tied together in your mind. Long-term financial planning may now be paying off, benefiting not just you but those closest, too.

WEDNESDAY, 11TH NOVEMBER
Moon square Venus

The atmosphere in your home and family is quite tense at the moment. This may be due to an outsider's interference in family business or a general level of disagreement within your personal circle. You cannot please everyone all the time, so try to keep the peace and wait for this influence to pass.

THURSDAY, 12TH NOVEMBER
Moon square Pluto

It's a tense day on the relationship front, and intense feelings may be bubbling up inside you or a lover. Resentment will be expressed today, but this isn't such a bad thing. It's only when issues aren't spoken about that problems begin. This could be a chance to clear the air.

FRIDAY, 13TH NOVEMBER
Jupiter direct

Your luck is about to change dramatically, particularly where business or money is concerned. You could see a truly wonderful opportunity now, but you won't be left to deal with it alone. You may, however, be content to organize your life and work by yourself, but be happy knowing that help is always an option.

SATURDAY, 14TH NOVEMBER
Sun sextile Mars

This should be an action-packed day around the home. You'll be eager to get your domestic environment spick and span and the whole family will be roped into this endeavour, whether they like it or not! Those who are considering a house move will find that this is the perfect day to get the ball rolling.

SUNDAY, 15TH NOVEMBER
Moon sextile Mercury

They say that it's easier to catch flies with honey than with vinegar. Well, you may not wish to catch any flies, but by following the general principle you will find it easier to get your own way now by using charm rather than shouting the odds at people. There is some good news in connection with money, but you may need to make a phone call or write a letter before you can get your hands on it.

MONDAY, 16TH NOVEMBER
Moon opposite Saturn

You may spend the day dashing around the countryside to help older relatives, particularly as you're the only one able to give them the practical support they need just now. You could also find that you are on a different wavelength from those whom you either live or work with.

TUESDAY, 17TH NOVEMBER
Venus into Sagittarius

The two themes that are likely to be important in the short-term future are those of children and having a good time. We hope that the two are compatible.

WEDNESDAY, 18TH NOVEMBER
Moon trine Jupiter

This is a day for good luck, good humour and a lot of laughs as the Moon makes a harmonious contact with Jupiter. Your home will provide the social setting for a gathering of the clans.

THURSDAY, 19TH NOVEMBER
New Moon

The New Moon in the area of domestic life and heritage shows that memories of childhood become very important now. Things learned then may now be questioned as you look back and try to relate happenings in early life to events today. You must admit that the world has changed immeasurably, so some concepts are rather dated. On the other hand, firm values passed down to you are as valid now as they ever were. Of course, you have to work out the difference for yourself.

FRIDAY, 20TH NOVEMBER
Mercury square Jupiter

There doesn't seem to be much fun about today. The atmosphere around you is tense and you may have problems weighing on your mind. If you suspect that you or your partner is running into money troubles, then stop now and do something about it. Taking firm action, however boring, is far better than worrying about a current or potential debt.

SATURDAY, 21ST NOVEMBER
Mercury retrograde

Whenever Mercury turns retrograde, muddle and misunderstandings abound. Things get held up in the post and vital bits of paper seem to vanish off the face of the earth. The car is likely to play up, and the computer or any other machinery that you have to deal with will join in. Communications will be tricky over the next few weeks; however, in time you may find ways around it.

SUNDAY, 22ND NOVEMBER
Sun into Sagittarius

The Sun's movement into your fifth Solar house shows that you've had enough of being dutiful and working your fingers to the bone. You now desperately need some fun. It won't do you any harm at all to please yourself over the next month, so think of something you really enjoy and go for it. Artistic ventures of all kinds, whether dramatic, poetic, literary or just the love of a good film, should be followed up. Indulge yourself to the hilt – you'll feel all the better for it.

MONDAY, 23RD NOVEMBER
Venus conjunct Pluto

You have enough glamour and charisma to have them falling in the aisles today! Take yourself off to the nearest party and live it up. All who set eyes on you will love and admire you.

TUESDAY, 24TH NOVEMBER
Moon sextile Sun

This is a good time for your love life. If you are in a committed relationship, then share quality time with your partner. If you're single, then today could bring you into contact with someone who will become very important romantically.

WEDNESDAY, 25TH NOVEMBER
Venus sextile Uranus

This should be an exciting day, especially if you happen to be male. There's a hint of amorous naughtiness about you and there should be the chance for some wickedness before the day is out. Of course women don't lose out completely, it's just that you are usually more sensible!

THURSDAY, 26TH NOVEMBER
Moon sextile Saturn

You and your lover seem to be in a strangely spiritual mood today. Neither of you feels like dealing with practical matters and you may be better off doing something completely different. Commune with nature by taking a walk in the woods or a stroll along the beach, or pay a visit to your local church or temple.

FRIDAY, 27TH NOVEMBER
Neptune into Aquarius

The distant and slow-moving planet, Neptune, enters your Solar house of relationships today. This is a long-term influence that will put you more in tune with your life partner. An intuitive sense of right or indeed wrong will soon become evident, and your reaction to this will be important.

SATURDAY, 28TH NOVEMBER
Mars trine Neptune

A kindly act by a co-worker will point you in the direction of added income today. This alone would usually convince you that not everyone is out for themselves, but today the whole atmosphere is one of consideration and shared effort. If you unite with colleagues you may find that you sacrifice a short-term advantage, but will gain in the long run – in terms of money and respect.

SUNDAY, 29TH NOVEMBER
Sun conjunct Pluto

What a day! You could fall head over heels in love with a delightful stranger and it's possible that you may be on the receiving end of a real windfall now, too. Love, creativity and pleasure should be top of the menu.

MONDAY, 30TH NOVEMBER
Moon conjunct Saturn

You may have some kind of legal or official matter to deal with and, as this seems to have some kind of long-term significance, it's best to tackle it now rather than allow it to slide. Some of you may be involved in education and this too needs thinking about, but equally you could be making plans for someone else.

December at a Glance

LOVE	❤		❤		❤		❤	
WORK	★		★		★			
MONEY	£		£					
HEALTH	✚		✚		✚		✚	
LUCK	☋		☋		☋		☋		☋

TUESDAY, 1ST DECEMBER
Mercury sextile Uranus

If you've been tongue-tied when trying to express yourself, you should be able to find the right words today. On the other hand, your lover may be tired of waiting for you and come up with the goods themselves!

WEDNESDAY, 2ND DECEMBER
Sun sextile Uranus

Friends will surprise you in the nicest possible way today. Single people who are reading this may suddenly discover that someone you considered as nothing more than a buddy is becoming far more important. A friend could introduce you to someone wonderful, or simply show you that they appreciate your friendship.

THURSDAY, 3RD DECEMBER
Full Moon

The Full Moon could make you feel a bit tetchy and tense and also bring you some sort of unexpected expense which, when you come to think of it, is probably only to be expected. The best thing to do today is to stick to your usual routine and not start anything new or important. Jog along and don't get caught up in anyone else's bad mood.

FRIDAY, 4TH DECEMBER
Moon opposite Venus

Your friends may be less than helpful to you just now, and it's possible that a platonic relationship may take a romantic turn. A female friend may suddenly become jealous or spiteful towards you, and it's up to you to decide to placate this woman or to do without her rather dubious friendship altogether.

SATURDAY, 5TH DECEMBER
Mercury sextile Mars

There's no doubt that you're feeling particularly brave today. Decide what you want to accomplish early and then go out and do it! Nothing can stop you as long as you believe in yourself. You may be quite argumentative, but that's only because you won't put up with obstacles now.

SUNDAY, 6TH DECEMBER
Moon trine Jupiter

Focus your attention on any practical affairs that you may have neglected in recent weeks. The Lunar aspect to Jupiter puts you firmly in control now and able to deal with everything from the big picture in career affairs to the smallest detail of day-to-day life. The exuberance of the giant planet enables you to cheerfully undertake arduous tasks and accomplish them with ease.

MONDAY, 7TH DECEMBER
Moon sextile Mars

This is a good day to go shopping for any form of transport, from renting a set of skis for your winter holiday to buying a new car. The same goes for any kind of tools, especially if they move along in some way, like a jigsaw or even a chisel. If you have to travel by public transport, you may find a better route for your usual journeys.

TUESDAY, 8TH DECEMBER
Moon trine Sun

The Lunar aspect to the Sun throws away all care and encourages you to have a good time. Social life will be a superb arena for you to show off your dazzling personality. This is no time for solitary activities of any kind; circulate with friends, and romance will enter your life.

WEDNESDAY, 9TH DECEMBER
Venus trine Saturn

This is an excellent time to go on a shopping trip with your lover. It won't matter if you buy anything or not as the outing will be enjoyable anyway, and that's the main purpose of the journey.

THURSDAY, 10TH DECEMBER
Moon square Sun

Boredom is your big problem today and you'll be tempted to lift yourself out of your languor by dipping into your pocket for a good night out or the odd treat or two. Breaking the bank isn't your intent, so don't go mad with the cash card. A demanding child may nag you to provide a toy or fashion item that'll hold the initial appeal for all of five minutes, so don't give in.

FRIDAY, 11TH DECEMBER
Venus into Capricorn

Any squabbles at work should be resolved by the entry of Venus into your Solar house of habits, effort and service to others. Colleagues will get on better with each other from now on, for a spirit of harmony is as important in the workplace as in your home. If you're self-employed or earn your living by means of your wits, the presence of Venus is very encouraging for your future prospects. You'll find that the influence of women takes on added importance from now on.

SATURDAY, 12TH DECEMBER
Mars sextile Pluto

Good news, a lot of flirtation and possibly an invitation to a surprise party is on the cards for today! It's one of those times when you should go with your impulses and please yourself, because everyone else is going to be pleased as well!

SUNDAY, 13TH DECEMBER
Moon sextile Sun

You're in a happy mood and determined to have some fun. There's a party atmosphere with plenty to be thankful about, and a fair dose of flirtation could be on the cards, too.

MONDAY, 14TH DECEMBER
Moon sextile Venus

This is a great day to spend gossiping with women friends or wandering around the shops spending money on small luxuries. Unfortunately, work and responsibilities will crowd in all to soon and spoil your pleasure. You may have to rush to get work done before you can get out and enjoy yourself or, alternatively, you could have to catch up with the chores after all your pleasant outings.

TUESDAY, 15TH DECEMBER
Mars trine Uranus

A minor argument could have a good outcome today since it will reveal the underlying reasons for disharmony within a close relationship. This is your chance to face up to the issues involved and, hopefully, resolve them.

LEO

WEDNESDAY, 16TH DECEMBER
Moon sextile Neptune
You will understand others far beyond the call of duty today. In fact, your intuitive sense will often be more instructive than the spoken word. In particular, those who work in an advisory capacity will reap the benefits of swift perception.

THURSDAY, 17TH DECEMBER
Moon sextile Uranus
If you are bored and lonely, then ring up a couple of your friends, because they are probably in much the same mood as yourself. If you all meet and do something on an impromptu basis, you will probably end up having the time of your lives. A friend could introduce you to a new face who may be destined to become an important part of your future.

FRIDAY, 18TH DECEMBER
New Moon
This month's New Moon is in an area of your chart that deals with creativity, so if there is something you want to do in the artistic field then this is the time to get started. For some of you this could be as important as making a home, starting a family or beginning a new business enterprise. Younger members of the family could also show signs of creative ability now.

SATURDAY, 19TH DECEMBER
Sun trine Saturn
A heady intellectual debate with an older person will be very enjoyable today. You could find that your respect for this person grows as minutes become hours. This could be the start of a lasting friendship with someone who will prove to be a good adviser.

SUNDAY, 20TH DECEMBER
Moon square Mars
Intuition and logic are battling for supremacy in your mind at the moment. You simply know that something is right but you are finding it hard to prove this to your own satisfaction, let alone anyone else's. If you have to choose, follow your intuition.

MONDAY, 21ST DECEMBER
Mercury conjunct Pluto
Today's influence favours child-centred activity, so if you want to conceive a child, find the right school for one or make any kind of positive moves in connection with younger members of your circle, then this is a good time to do it.

TUESDAY, 22ND DECEMBER
Sun into Capricorn

The movement of the Sun into your Solar sixth house of work signals a period of success in your endeavours. Whatever you do will have a patina of success and glamour about it and you will be the envy of other less fortunate or hard-working souls. Don't allow their envy to diminish your confidence.

WEDNESDAY, 23RD DECEMBER
Mercury sextile Uranus

For some, today brings a declaration of undying love. However, for most of you it signals a time of flirtation, amorous entanglement and blissful seduction. Either way, we doubt that you'll complain!

THURSDAY, 24TH DECEMBER
Moon square Pluto

Something may go strangely wrong with your sex life today. It could be one of those occasions when either you or your partner simply can't turn it on. Alternatively, you may both be trying too hard to impress each other, wearing yourselves out without really enjoying the experience. Relax for a while and try not to make such a production of lovemaking. Listen to some music together, share a glass of wine and then let everything take its course – if it wants to.

FRIDAY, 25TH DECEMBER
Moon conjunct Jupiter

If you have ever put yourself out for others, such as giving money to charity or taking on voluntary work, then this Christmas Day providence will pay you back. You are due for some kind of karmic reward; you may not be thanked by the same people whom you helped, and thanks may come in an unexpected way, but something good is certainly on the horizon.

SATURDAY, 26TH DECEMBER
Moon square Sun

The drudgery of day-to-day life will not be your cup of tea now and you'd give a lot to be flying off to an exotic paradise. Even if you can't manage this, you can always dream. Come back to earth gently!

SUNDAY, 27TH DECEMBER
Moon square Venus

Examine your beliefs today, because you may discover that your philosophy of life differs from that of the people around you. This may be no bad thing; after all, you are an independent individual and therefore entitled to believe whatever you want. However, you may simply have to accept that you're on a different wavelength from the rest of your community.

MONDAY, 28TH DECEMBER
Mercury sextile Mars

For the intellectually inclined this is going to be a great day. Lots of fun is on offer, especially if you're feeling competitive. Word games, enjoyable arguments and debates should feature, and passionate declarations are possible if you're wooing the object of your affections.

TUESDAY, 29TH DECEMBER
Saturn direct

Saturn turns to direct motion today in your ninth Solar house. This will speed up any pending legal matters and help you complete any long and arduous task that you have set yourself. You may need to travel on business or for social purposes over the next few months.

WEDNESDAY, 30TH DECEMBER
Moon trine Neptune

Your mood is spiritual and romantic rather than practical or money-minded today, and your dreams will take you to realms that you never thought possible. You may try your hand at astral travelling – as long as you know how to get back inside your body again! You may dream of falling in love, or simply spend an evening watching television and drooling over your favourite film star.

THURSDAY, 31ST DECEMBER
Moon trine Mars

Men in your life gain added importance on the last day of 1998. Talking things over with a male friend will clarify your thoughts no end. You may find that you reveal your true dreams to this person, and find that he is in tune with you. This bodes well for the future in 1999. Happy New Year!

1999

January at a Glance

LOVE	❤	❤	❤	❤	❤
WORK	★	★	★	★	★
MONEY	£				
HEALTH	✚	✚	✚	✚	
LUCK	U	U	U		

FRIDAY, 1ST JANUARY
Mercury square Jupiter

There doesn't seem to be much fun about on the first day of the year. This astrological aspect always spells tension and problems for you. Be on the lookout for money troubles for you or your partner, and make a decision to do something about this. Taking firm action, however boring this is, is far better than worrying yourself sick over a current or potential debt situation.

SATURDAY, 2ND JANUARY
Full Moon

Apart from a slightly frustrating Full Moon situation today, there is not much going on in the planetary firmament. The best thing to do is to stick to your usual way of doing things and to avoid starting anything new or important. If you feel off-colour or out of sorts, then take whatever medicines you need and try not to work too hard.

SUNDAY, 3RD JANUARY
Moon opposite Venus

Emotional anxieties come to the fore today, but if you were honest you'd have to admit that you're being slightly neurotic over this. It's all the fault of the Lunar opposition to Venus which has managed to both heighten your emotional vulnerability and sap your energy levels at the same time. This problem of tiredness occurs again and again so perhaps a visit to your medical practitioner would be in order.

MONDAY, 4TH JANUARY
Venus into Aquarius

Venus, the planet or romance, moves into your horoscopic area of close relationships from today increasing your physical desires and bringing the light of love into your heart. If you're involved in a long-term partnership, this brings a chance to renew the magic of the early days of your union. If single, then the next few weeks should bring a stunning new attraction into your life.

TUESDAY, 5TH JANUARY
Venus conjunct Neptune

What a lovely, romantic day this is! You and your lover ought to get out of the house and away from the chores if you can and take a stroll in the fresh air. A beach or the countryside would certainly provide the right atmosphere. Try to go out later in the day to a dance or for a nice meal somewhere special and, of course, try to fit in a bit of love-making somewhere along the line.

WEDNESDAY, 6TH JANUARY
Moon square Pluto

You know what you want but it seems to be very difficult for you to get your hands on it. You probably can't afford to finance the lifestyle that you want so badly, but even if you could afford it in theory there are more important demands being made on your finances just now. A spiteful or jealous person may irritate or upset you today.

THURSDAY, 7TH JANUARY
Mercury into Capricorn

The movement of Mercury into your Solar sixth house of work, duties and health suggests that a slightly more serious phase is on the way. Over the next three weeks or so you will have to concentrate on what needs to be done rather than on having a good time. You may have a fair bit to do with neighbours, colleagues and relatives of around your own age group soon and you will have to spend a fair bit of time on the phone to them.

FRIDAY, 8TH JANUARY
Moon trine Venus

Social opportunities are all around you now, so don't sit around on you own when there are people out there who'd welcome your company. Pop into a neglected friend's for a cup of tea and a chat; you'll be glad you made the effort as well as cheering up someone who needs it. Pick up the phone and ring a distant friend or one or two of your relatives for a good old gossip today.

LEO

SATURDAY, 9TH JANUARY
Moon square Sun

It wouldn't be a good idea to overload your schedule too much today. We know that you're bounding with self-confidence but the vitality levels just aren't up to it at the moment. If you're working, the evening won't come around fast enough. If not, then leave domestic chores for now. A few unwashed dishes aren't the end of the world.

SUNDAY, 10TH JANUARY
Moon opposite Saturn

You may have to rush around the countryside in order to sort out problems that are coming at you from the direction of the older members of your family. Your parents may need practical help of some kind and you may be the only one who is around to deal with this at the moment. You may also find that you are on a different wavelength from those whom you either live or work with now.

MONDAY, 11TH JANUARY
Moon square Uranus

There will be tension in the family today and you look likely to become stuck in the middle of it. Your partner may fall out with one of your parents or a parent may fall out with someone else in the family. Older people, those who are in positions of authority and parental figures generally, could be in a tense and tetchy mood today.

TUESDAY, 12TH JANUARY
Venus sextile Pluto

You should be trembling with barely suppressed passion for much of the day. Venus has a marvellous aspect to Pluto which brings deep feelings bubbling to the surface. If you can't sweep the love of your life off his or her feet today, then you aren't really trying! You have an intensity and a magnetism that's very appealing!

WEDNESDAY, 13TH JANUARY
Venus conjunct Uranus

You could find the love of your life today! This is a truly spectacular time, especially in connection with love and romance. Perhaps your lover will go down on one knee and pop the question and, if so, he or she will do so in the most romantic manner possible. Your partner may have great news for you and he or she may surprise you by coming home with an unusual gift.

THURSDAY, 14TH JANUARY
Sun sextile Jupiter

Money luck is forecast as the Sun moves into excellent aspect to Jupiter. If you are seeking employment, then the chances are good that you'll find a position that is both suitable and profitable today. Work affairs generally are favourable, and your health should be in tip-top condition.

FRIDAY, 15TH JANUARY
Sun square Mars

More haste means less speed when the Sun and Mars move into such a trying aspect. Arguments are likely and very little can be accomplished when everyone seems to be pulling in opposite directions at once. If you slow down and think things through, many of these problems can be solved before they arise.

SATURDAY, 16TH JANUARY
Moon conjunct Mercury

When the Moon makes contact with Mercury the mental powers are enhanced. You're very sharp now especially when you have to deal with any technicalities of life. If you're dealing with tradesmen, plumbers, domestic engineers and the like, you're very sharp. Unfortunately since the Solar house of health is also activated you may be prone to hypochondria today. More realistically, you may even suffer from some allergy or other; if in doubt, consult your doctor.

SUNDAY, 17TH JANUARY
New Moon

Today's New Moon gives you the stamina to shrug off any minor ailments that have been troubling you. Occurring, as it does, in your Solar house of health and work, it's obvious that you need to get yourself into shape to face the challenges that await you. A few early nights, a better diet and a readiness to give up bad habits such as smoking, will work wonders.

MONDAY, 18TH JANUARY
Sun square Saturn

You may have an opportunity now to travel in connection with work, but this may not turn out to be as easy at it looks. If you do go away on any kind of business matter now, make sure that you have every contingency covered and that you allow plenty of time for delays and setbacks. Make sure that you allow plenty of time for all your appointments, whether these involve travel or not.

TUESDAY, 19TH JANUARY
Moon conjunct Venus

If you are a man or if you are reading this on behalf of a man, you can expect something very romantic and pleasant to happen. If you happen to be a woman, then you can expect to have some kind of pleasant social event in the company of other women today. All working relationships, partnerships, marriage or other personal relationships will be well starred today.

WEDNESDAY, 20TH JANUARY
Sun into Aquarius

The Sun moves into the area of your chart devoted to relationships from today. If things have been difficult in a partnership, either personal or in business, then this is your chance to put everything back into its proper place. It's obvious that the significant other in your life deserves respect and affection and that's just what you're now prepared to give. Teamwork is the key to success over the next month.

THURSDAY, 21ST JANUARY
Mars opposite Saturn

A difference of opinion could easily escalate into full-scale war today if you aren't careful. It may be a minor matter, but there will be a tendency to blow even the most trivial dispute into a feud. Take care while travelling too, because your temper will be heating up.

FRIDAY, 22ND JANUARY
Sun conjunct Neptune

You'll possess an intuitive, almost psychic awareness of the feelings of those close to you today. The rapport you experience with your partner will verge on the telepathic. This is reassuring since you are both so much in tune with each other.

SATURDAY, 23RD JANUARY
Mercury sextile Jupiter

You will probably need to ask for some help with a tricky task today and, if so, you will get the assistance you require. You may be struggling with some kind of communications machinery or maybe it is a prescription for medicine that you don't understand. Another possibility is that you need advice over a financial matter, but whatever the problem is you will find the right person to answer it.

SUNDAY, 24TH JANUARY
Mercury square Saturn

You may begin to take an interest in health and healing today and this includes being introduced to the idea of spiritual or 'Reiki healing'. It may be astrology that captures your attention, or maybe some other form of esoteric system of character analysis and predictive techniques will start to fascinate you.

MONDAY, 25TH JANUARY
Moon square Uranus

A sudden and unexpected event will make it impossible for you to get to a meeting of some kind today. You will have to take over from someone else due to circumstances that are beyond everyone's control. This may put you in the hot seat for a while but it may also do you good in an off-beat way. It may be that this problem also gives you an opportunity to try your hand at doing something outside of your usual routine.

TUESDAY, 26TH JANUARY
Mars into Scorpio

Your energies will be directed to your home and the area around it. Thus you may spend time working on or in the home or on the land around the place today. If the dishes are piling up in the kitchen, then get down to washing them up and if you haven't a clean shirt or a pair of socks to match, then get around to doing the washing now. Mars in the domestic area of your life over the next few weeks could bring a rash of plumbers, builders and all kinds of other domestic workmen your way.

WEDNESDAY, 27TH JANUARY
Venus sextile Saturn

This is a slow time and that is no bad thing. At least you will have the time to think, plan and generally get your mind into gear, ready for the opportunities and challenges that lie ahead. A foreigner or someone who has recently travelled abroad could change the romantic direction of your thoughts.

THURSDAY, 28TH JANUARY
Venus into Pisces

Venus enters the area of your chart that is closely involved with love and sex today. Oddly enough, this aspect can bring the end of a difficult relationship, or just as easily begin a wonderful new one. If you have been dating but haven't got around to 'mating', this could be the start of something wonderful. Your emotional life over the next two or three weeks should be something to remember, that's for sure!

FRIDAY, 29TH JANUARY
Venus trine Mars

A sense of harmony and peace returns to the workplace as all discontents are soothed away by a few calming words and a display of care. In some cases, there'll be a hint of romance in the most mundane surroundings. In health matters too, any overstress or irritating ailments would benefit from a calmer, more serene atmosphere. It looks like an all-round good day, because cash worries too will be eased.

SATURDAY, 30TH JANUARY
Sun sextile Pluto

There may be astonishing news today and the chances are that one of your friends is the bearer of these unusual tidings. You may be asked to attend a particularly glamorous event or join others in a prestigious business matter.

SUNDAY, 31ST JANUARY
Full Moon eclipse

There is a Full Moon eclipse in your own sign today and this will bring your current lifestyle sharply into focus for you to concentrate on. You may have misjudged a situation or you may have taken some kind of wrong road recently, therefore give a bit of thought to what you are trying to do with your life and where you must go from here on. You may be irritated with yourself for being foolish in some way. Eclipses can be quite difficult to live with for a while.

February at a Glance

LOVE	❤	❤	❤	❤	❤
WORK	★	★			
MONEY	£	£	£	£	
HEALTH	✚				
LUCK	U	U			

MONDAY, 1ST FEBRUARY
Mars square Neptune

Before you provide a surprise for your family or spouse, it might be a good idea to check out what it is exactly that they want! You could so easily do the wrong thing and end up pleasing nobody!

TUESDAY, 2ND FEBRUARY
Sun conjunct Uranus

If you thought that you knew your partner inside out, prepare to be astonished by a surprise that someone special springs on you. If you aren't romantically involved at present, then Cupid's dart could strike at any moment.

WEDNESDAY, 3RD FEBRUARY
Sun conjunct Mercury

You and your lover have a great deal to talk over and today is the day to do it. If you are in the early stages of a relationship, you will find that you have a great deal in common and you will be able to while away many happy hours together discussing your childhoods and backgrounds. If you have something that is niggling you, you should not keep this to yourself because it will linger there, possibly causing long-term resentment.

THURSDAY, 4TH FEBRUARY
Moon opposite Jupiter

Don't take any chances with money today. Keep to the tried and tested paths and don't take decisions that you haven't really thought through properly. You may find that a partner or a close associate needs some extra financial help and this could put a strain on your savings. Legal or official matters may be difficult to handle today and if it is at all possible, try to avoid tackling these now.

FRIDAY, 5TH FEBRUARY
Mercury conjunct Uranus

Your mind is working at a rate of knots today and your ideas are extremely inventive and original. If you do happen to find yourself short of a notion or two, ask one of your close friends because they'll have the answer.

SATURDAY, 6TH FEBRUARY
Venus square Pluto

It's an intense day emotionally speaking. Venus squares Pluto making the whole question of feelings and desires difficult to deal with. Of course this could set you off on a passionate course with no thought to consequences, but it could also bring far more disturbing feelings and resentments to the surface. If there's a financial worry in the background, this too could emerge as a disruption within your relationships.

LEO

SUNDAY, 7TH FEBRUARY
Moon conjunct Mars

Something will take you back to revisit your past today. You may bump into an old flame and take time out to talk about times gone by, or you may find yourself back in a part of town that you haven't been near for years. Something may help you to come to terms with old hurts and disappointments once and for all today.

MONDAY, 8TH FEBRUARY
Moon square Sun

You aren't in the most active of moods today. The Moon's square aspect to the Sun ensures that you'll be happiest within your home environment. You won't want to tax your system at all, so a day of lounging about is your idea of bliss. Of course, there are domestic duties too, but you're likely to rely on the goodwill of your other half to carry out those. Don't be surprised if your lazy attitude is resented.

TUESDAY, 9TH FEBRUARY
Moon trine Jupiter

Your home and domestic circumstances are really rather good now and whatever you have in mind will go particularly well today. You may be keen to move house or to put your own home into some kind of new order and this is the time to get all this into action. Your partner will have good news in connection with money or business matters and this too will help to ease any financial burdens in the home.

WEDNESDAY, 10TH FEBRUARY
Moon sextile Uranus

It looks as though you've discovered the fountain of eternal youth today, because you've got a spring in your step and a song in your heart. It's got to be love that's lifted your spirits and renewed your joy in life. Serious concerns can be forgotten for a while because you're set on a fun-filled course. Those who are single will suddenly encounter someone who is destined to hold a special place in their heart.

THURSDAY, 11TH FEBRUARY
Mercury sextile Saturn

Today is good for business travel and also for anything connected with educational affairs. If travelling in company, you can be assured of a chatty and enjoyable time. If you are lucky, you could encounter someone who will become the love of your life in an institution such as a library or college.

FRIDAY, 12TH FEBRUARY
Mercury into Pisces

Mercury moves into one of the most sensitive areas of your chart from today. Anything of an intimate nature from your physical relationships to the state of your bank balance comes under scrutiny now. Turn your heightened perceptions to your love life, important partnerships and any affair that deals with investment, insurance, tax or shared resources. An intelligent approach now will save you a lot of problems later.

SATURDAY, 13TH FEBRUARY
Jupiter into Aries

Jupiter moves into its own natural home today, giving you a yearning for adventure beyond the present narrow confines of your life. For many, this will mean travel to far-off exotic places in order to experience cultures, thoughts and attitudes that are different from your own.

SUNDAY, 14TH FEBRUARY
Moon sextile Jupiter

It's an apt St Valentine's Day since you and your lover seem to be happy to do things together. You are both on the same wavelength now and your dreams and ideas seem to be much the same as each other's. For once the pressures of the world won't tend to drive you apart.

MONDAY, 15TH FEBRUARY
Moon conjunct Uranus

Other people will take you by surprise today and this may have the effect of stirring up your emotions in a big way. You could find yourself being courted by a fascinating member of the opposite sex. You may find that the lover you thought you could depend upon starts to act in a strangely disconcerting manner. Friends and colleagues may also do odd things today.

TUESDAY, 16TH FEBRUARY
New Moon eclipse

Today's eclipse marks a major turning point in your life and this should turn your relationships inside out. If you are heavily influenced by other signs or planets, then the changes which are whirling around in your life may affect some other area of your life rather than the partnership one. However, others of you can expect a real make-or-break atmosphere in your love life now.

LEO

WEDNESDAY, 17TH FEBRUARY
Sun sextile Saturn

Your partner could express a desire to travel today. Though there are plenty of restrictions in your lives at the moment, this might not be such a bad idea. In fact, if you think about the possibility seriously, you'll probably find that it's not such a far-fetched one after all.

THURSDAY, 18TH FEBRUARY
Mercury square Pluto

Dealings with youngsters could be fraught with worries today for you have some dark suspicions concerning an offspring. It may be that there's no substance to your anxiety, yet it isn't a thing that you can ignore. Don't shy away from enforcing house rules, or setting limits to behaviour. It's just another way of expressing your love.

FRIDAY, 19TH FEBRUARY
Sun into Pisces

Today, the Sun enters your Solar eighth house of beginnings and endings. Thus, over the next month, you can expect something to wind its way to a conclusion, while something else starts to take its place. This doesn't seem to signify a major turning point or any really big event in your life but it does mark one of those small turning points that we all go through from time to time.

SATURDAY, 20TH FEBRUARY
Void Moon

This is one of those days when none of the planets is making any worthwhile kind of aspect to any of the others. Even the Moon is 'void of course', which means that it is not making any aspects of any importance to any of the other planets. On such a day, avoid starting anything new and don't set out to do anything important. Do what needs to be done and take some time off for a rest.

SUNDAY, 21ST FEBRUARY
Venus into Aries

Venus enters your Solar ninth house of exploration this month and this may make you slightly restless. Venus is concerned with the pleasures of life and also with leisure activities of all kinds, so explore such ideas as your sporting interests, or perhaps of listening to interesting music or going to art galleries and the like. You may want to travel somewhere new and interesting soon.

LEO

MONDAY, 22ND FEBRUARY
Venus sextile Neptune

A dissatisfaction with the familiar scene is developing in your life. You want new horizons and to experience the exotic. Many will want to travel especially to places where there is a lot of water. Perhaps a cruise would fit the bill. Others will be more interested in exercising artistic talents.

TUESDAY, 23RD FEBRUARY
Moon opposite Pluto

People need your help today. Whether the issues involve friends with emotional problems, or teenagers with educational difficulties the problems will be pressing. Even though you have enough on your plate at the moment, you won't be able to turn your back on a heartfelt plea for assistance. You have to be patient today even if there's little you can actually do. Perhaps a sympathetic shoulder to cry on is all that's needed.

WEDNESDAY, 24TH FEBRUARY
Venus conjunct Jupiter

A conjunction of the two beneficial planets, Venus and Jupiter, must herald a fortunate day. When this occurs in the area of adventure and travel, it's obvious that attraction of foreign cultures and far-off places are the order of the day. It's also a time to be friendly, show kindness even to strangers now because the smallest gesture of concern will be amply repaid. It's a day to take the wider view and not get bogged down in details.

THURSDAY, 25TH FEBRUARY
Moon trine Sun

Today you just know that you are right! Your confidence will be on a real high and you will be absolutely sure that you are on the right track. A romance or relationship will begin to move into a much better mode now and you have a real chance of sorting out any misunderstandings that have arisen between you. You will be able to explain how you feel to your lover and you will have an almost psychic understanding of his or her needs.

FRIDAY, 26TH FEBRUARY
Sun trine Mars

Some serious action is required concerning your financial state. When it comes to loans, investments, pensions and all other matters concerning 'tied up' money, playing for time won't do any good at all. Make a decisive move now and ensure a prosperous future!

SATURDAY, 27TH FEBRUARY
Jupiter sextile Neptune

Today's rare aspect between Jupiter and Neptune may not bring a direct influence on your own life; however you will feel the effects through events in the lives of close friends or a partner. There may be a closer understanding now, as good fortune smiles on someone that you care about.

SUNDAY, 28TH FEBRUARY
Moon opposite Uranus

You may have thought that you'd covered every topic that your partner could come up with, that you are intimately aware of every personal idiosyncrasy and defect, but you're in for a surprise today! Your other half is about to say or do something totally out of character. Don't be too shocked, this could open a whole new and exciting chapter in the history of your relationship.

March at a Glance

LOVE	❤	❤	❤	❤	
WORK	★	★	★	★	★
MONEY	£				
HEALTH	✪	✪	✪	✪	
LUCK	♘	♘	♘		

MONDAY, 1ST MARCH
Saturn into Taurus

Your career moves to centre stage today with the probability that certain changes in the workplace have put you on edge. You may think the future is less certain than it was, with all the financial insecurity that that implies.

TUESDAY, 2ND MARCH
Mercury into Aries

Mercury enters your Solar house of adventure on philosophy from today and stimulates your curiosity. Everything from international affairs to religious questions will tax your mind. Your desire to travel will be boosted for a few weeks, as indeed will a need to expand your knowledge, perhaps by taking up a course at a local college. Keep an open mind. Allow yourself encounters with new ideas.

WEDNESDAY, 3RD MARCH
Venus trine Pluto

You are extremely original and creative today. However, you shouldn't expect others to understand you since the depth of your feelings will be expressed in anything you do. On the other hand, you are fulfilling your own sense of values, so other people's opinions shouldn't come into the picture.

THURSDAY, 4TH MARCH
Venus sextile Uranus

Great news from someone who is at a distance from you will cheer you up today. If you have been parted from someone you love, you will soon be able to be with them once again.

FRIDAY, 5TH MARCH
Mercury sextile Neptune

When it comes to romantic fantasies, this is the day! If your lover is far away, then a long phone call or a good old-fashioned love-letter is an excellent idea. If that's not the case, then lose yourself in a bodice-ripping novel or TV weepie!

SATURDAY, 6TH MARCH
Moon square Neptune

Nothing is as it seems today. If your partner or a family member seems distant and cold, remember that appearances are deceptive and that there may be a secret worry behind this apparent indifference.

SUNDAY, 7TH MARCH
Moon square Uranus

Not a day for planning anything because your other half will have totally different inclinations from your own. Some friction may occur but you can be sure that this will not be too serious.

MONDAY, 8TH MARCH
Moon trine Venus

The Lunar aspect to Venus puts a romantic spark in your soul today. There's nothing you'd like better than an intimate *tête-à-tête* with someone you love. Forget your worries and take that special person in your life out for a night of glamour. If you are single, go for glamour anyway. Someone will catch your eye.

LEO

TUESDAY, 9TH MARCH
Moon trine Jupiter

A convivial atmosphere takes hold as the Moon contacts Jupiter, spreading a little happiness around you. Negative moods are now forgiven and forgotten as harmonious influences lift your spirits. You could make a special effort to show the more romantic side to your nature and take some time out for an intimate celebration to remember.

WEDNESDAY, 10TH MARCH
Mercury retrograde

When Mercury goes into backward motion the outlook is generally disrupted. This time, the area of concern is travel, holidays and foreign affairs. Nothing will go to plan for a few weeks, but don't despair, you can avoid a lot of problems by double-checking all arrangements once again just to be on the safe side.

THURSDAY, 11TH MARCH
Moon square Mercury

Don't be too hard on yourself today. Accept that you have probably been working hard or that you have been under too much stress for your own good. Nobody can do everything and you are not superman (or superwoman, for that matter), so you shouldn't expect so much of yourself. You may have to spend some time with a colleague who is going through a crisis today.

FRIDAY, 12TH MARCH
Moon sextile Mars

The accent is on your personal security today. Home-based matters such as redecoration, DIY endeavours or furniture replacement may be desirable but all cost money. The stars promise that you will fulfil your wishes, but only at the cost of some self-denial. Patience is desperately needed now. Rome wasn't built in a day, and a perfect home isn't likely to be either.

SATURDAY, 13TH MARCH
Mercury sextile Neptune

This is a time when your capacity for romantic fantasy sweeps away any vestige of common sense. Forget the phone bill because you'll be happy to keep your lover on the end of the line for hours.

LEO

SUNDAY, 14TH MARCH
Mercury sextile Pluto

Other people seem to be making all the decisions and all the running lately and, while this may leave you feeling a little helpless, it could well work in your favour. Therefore, if others want to do all your thinking and deciding for you today, let them!

MONDAY, 15TH MARCH
Moon sextile Venus

The love life is emphasized under the marvellous aspect between the Moon and Venus. This could be the start of a new and very important relationship or just a renewal of ties that have become a matter of habit. The bonds of affection and attraction are very strong. Expressions of love will be easily and sincerely made now. The more creative souls are particularly favoured under such fortunate stars.

TUESDAY, 16TH MARCH
Moon square Pluto

You are trying to achieve love, understanding and blessed harmony all around you today and the chances are that you are directing most of your efforts towards your partner. All this would be wonderful if it actually worked, but today, for some unknown reason, all your efforts will come to naught. Worse still, your motives could be misinterpreted, leading to all kinds of unfair and untrue accusations.

WEDNESDAY, 17TH MARCH
New Moon

Apart from a New Moon today, there are no major planetary happenings. This suggests that you avoid making major changes in your life just now but make a couple of fresh starts in very minor matters. You may feel like taking your partner to task over their irritating ways, but perhaps today is not the best day for doing this.

THURSDAY, 18TH MARCH
Venus into Taurus

Venus moves into your Solar house of ambition and prominence from today. If you're involved in any career in the arts, beautification, entertainment or public relations, then you're bound to do well over the next few weeks. Those who work for women bosses won't do badly either since a female influence in the workplace will aid your ambitions. Since Venus is the planet of charisma use diplomacy to solve professional problems. You can hardly fail to win with such a capacity for charm.

FRIDAY, 19TH MARCH
Sun conjunct Mercury

Approach contracts and agreements with caution today. That's not to say that they are bad things to get involved with, just that you've got to play your cards close to your chest to make the most of them. You have the ability to handle any negotiations with ease since your shrewd appreciation of realities gives you the edge over any opponents. You'll have no trouble with small print.

SATURDAY, 20TH MARCH
Venus conjunct Saturn

Today's aspect between Venus and Saturn may not be one of the most vibrant and interesting but it is very good for your worldly prospects. The help of older females will aid you in everything from a career search to setting up your own business. Anything connected with cosmetics, art and horticulture should benefit now.

SUNDAY, 21ST MARCH
Sun into Aries

The Sun moves into your Solar ninth house today and it will stay there for a month. This would be a good time to travel overseas or to explore new neighbourhoods. It is also a good time to take up an interest in spiritual matters. You may find yourself keen to read about religious or philosophical subjects or even to explore the world of psychic healing over the next month or so.

MONDAY, 22ND MARCH
Moon trine Neptune

Your mood is spiritual and romantic rather than practical or money-minded today and your dreams will take you to realms that you never thought possible. You may try your hand at astral travelling – as long as you know how to make sure that you get back inside yourself again! You may dream of falling in love or you may spend an evening watching television and drooling over your favourite film star.

TUESDAY, 23RD MARCH
Venus square Neptune

It's going to be difficult to tell truth from fiction in all affairs of the heart today. You'll be prone to fears concerning the state of your relationship, or feel that you are being deceived in some way. Try not to take such thoughts seriously; there are just too many things you don't know at the moment, and fretting about them constantly isn't going to make your life any easier. This is another day when realism is vital.

LEO

WEDNESDAY, 24TH MARCH
Moon square Sun

It's a fairly mixed up day emotionally speaking for you feel somewhat vulnerable and not your usual outgoing self at all. Though the trends are generally good, you can't quite believe your luck and will be waiting for something to go wrong. There may also be vague suspicion about a friend's motives but don't do anything about it just yet.

THURSDAY, 25TH MARCH
Sun sextile Neptune

An intuitive understanding between yourself and your partner is possible now. You won't have to speak volumes to comprehend each other's point of view perfectly. This applies to professional partnerships as well as more personal links.

FRIDAY, 26TH MARCH
Moon square Saturn

You cannot get away with drifting and dreaming today because any number of important matters are crying out for your attention now. You may have to concentrate on a number of details and make sure that you have done everything that needs to be done before you can think of relaxing today. You could find yourself tied to the word processor or to the company books. (Jonathan and Sasha know just how this feels and can sympathize with you today!)

SATURDAY, 27TH MARCH
Venus opposite Mars

This is not going to be an easy day since demands will be made from both bosses and your family, usually at the same time. Attempts to be reasonable will meet with hostility so it'll be best if you keep your head down just now.

SUNDAY, 28TH MARCH
Void Moon

Occasionally one finds a day in which neither the planets nor the Moon make any major aspects to each other and on such a day the Moon's course is said to be 'void'. There is nothing wrong with a day like this but there is no point in trying to start anything new or anything important because there isn't enough of a planetary boost to get it off the ground. Stick to your normal routine.

MONDAY, 29TH MARCH
Moon square Pluto

Keep an eye on children and young people, they may have problems on their mind or they may simply need a bit more than the usual amount of love and attention. You may find yourself temporarily struggling with a creative project.

TUESDAY, 30TH MARCH
Jupiter trine Pluto

Today's optimistic combination of Jupiter and Pluto encourages you to take a chance! Though not in favour of gambling, we could suggest making a small wager. Travel affairs too are well starred. Perhaps it's time to take a holiday.

WEDNESDAY, 31ST MARCH
Full Moon

This is likely to be a really awkward day for the kind of travelling that you have to do. A vehicle could let you down just when you most need it or public transport that you usually rely on could suddenly disappear from the face of the earth.

April at a Glance

LOVE	❤	❤	❤	
WORK	★	★	★	
MONEY	£	£		
HEALTH	✚	✚	✚	
LUCK	♘	♘	♘	♘

THURSDAY, 1ST APRIL
Sun conjunct Jupiter

This is a day full of luck and happiness. The Sun meets up with Jupiter boosting your confidence and vision. A person you meet could well open your eyes to the possibilities and opportunities that surround you. You'll feel a sense of rightness with the universe that's almost religious in nature. All in all, a very good day.

FRIDAY, 2ND APRIL
Mercury direct

Mercury resumes its direct motion from today, so a lot of the confusions that have plagued joint finances and investments will now be ended. This would be a good day to cast your eye over all budgetary affairs to make sure that all is well.

LEO

SATURDAY, 3RD APRIL
Moon conjunct Mars

This could be another tense day around the home. The Lunar conjunction with Mars ensures that tempers are frayed and that feelings are running high. A lot of the fault will lie with you though, simply because you are being rather demanding at the moment and family members are becoming rather resentful of this tyranny. If you could learn to compromise a little, then you'd all get along far better.

SUNDAY, 4TH APRIL
Mercury sextile Venus

There's a highly romantic outlook today. The Lunar aspect to Venus puts you in a sentimental and loving frame of mind. You'll be anxious to share all spare time with a lover. If you're inclined to amorous conquest, you are guaranteed the response you desire. Your love life aside, those who are involved in delicate negotiations of any kind will find that diplomacy and charm will win the day.

MONDAY, 5TH APRIL
Moon sextile Neptune

For once the path of true love seems to be running smoothly. Whether you are engaged in a deep, passionate relationship or a mere flirtation, the outlook is excellent and promises a lot of fun.

TUESDAY, 6TH APRIL
Saturn square Neptune

A moody and an irascible day for you we're afraid. Saturn and Neptune are at odds bringing a lot of insecurities to the surface. The career picture is the main area of concern, but there may be worrying undercurrents in a close relationship too. Steady as you go!

WEDNESDAY, 7TH APRIL
Sun sextile Uranus

You could be invited to make an impromptu trip today. You need company though so get someone special to accompany you. If single, then there may be a hint of romance at the end of your journey.

THURSDAY, 8TH APRIL
Moon sextile Mars

If you have been feeling off-colour lately, you should now be feeling much better. Indeed, you may find that you have too much excess energy and that your bouncy mood irritates all who are around you. You will be able to get a number of household chores or do-it-yourself jobs out of the way with an amazing turn of speed and efficiency. Allow yourself to relax in the evening.

FRIDAY, 9TH APRIL
Moon sextile Mercury

As the Moon contacts Mercury it's time to put your cards on the table. A meeting will work in your favour if you are open and honest in your opinions now. Don't be afraid to stand out from the crowd.

SATURDAY, 10TH APRIL
Moon square Saturn

You may find considerable opposition to your plans today and it may be hard to get others to see your point of view. Your partner or lover could be strangely unwilling to take your part or to understand you today. You may find that your parents are out sympathy with you, while your colleagues and superiors at work could be truly obnoxious. Try staying in bed for the day!

SUNDAY, 11TH APRIL
Moon sextile Sun

You feel centred, happy and at peace with the world today and other people are as happy with you as you are with yourself. This is an excellent time to speak with in-laws and other relatives by marriage because they will be able to understand your point of view.

MONDAY, 12TH APRIL
Venus into Gemini

Venus moves into your eleventh house of friendship and group activities today, bringing a few weeks of happiness and harmony for you and your friends. You could fall in love under this transit or you could reaffirm your feelings towards a current partner. You should be looking and feeling rather good now but, if not, this is a good time to spend some money on your appearance and also to do something about any nagging health problems.

TUESDAY, 13TH APRIL
Moon sextile Venus

The link between the Moon and Venus adds a compelling and seductive quality to your nature now. Since you're quick on the uptake, it won't take you long to realize that you're in a position to twist anyone around your little finger. A small flirtation today will gain you far more than any number of confrontations.

LEO

WEDNESDAY, 14TH APRIL
Moon into Aries
The Moon is in the area of your chart that makes you want to reach out and to explore the world. You may feel restless or irritable with your lifestyle today but there is no point in trying to change it just now. There are no really important planetary movements going on today; therefore your best bet is to stick to your usual routine and put up with the boredom and restlessness for once.

THURSDAY, 15TH APRIL
Moon conjunct Jupiter
Though there might be a test of your self-belief at some point today it's important that you cling to your faith. The Moon conjuncts Jupiter now and lifts your mind out of a rut while setting your sights on affairs in distant parts of the world. You can't be bothered with petty worries and small-minded attitudes. You've got bigger, better concepts to dwell on.

FRIDAY, 16TH APRIL
New Moon
The New Moon in your house of adventure urges you to push ahead with new projects. You're in a self-confident mood, and feel able to tackle anything the world throws at you. There's a lure of the exotic today as well, as far-off places exert a powerful attraction. Think again about widening your personal horizons, by travel or, indeed, by taking up an educational course. Intellectually you're on top form and your curiosity is boundless.

SATURDAY, 17TH APRIL
Mercury into Aries
You should take every opportunity that you can to gather facts, information, impressions and evidence today before going ahead with anything. You may have to deal with legal or official matters now and, if so, having all the right information to hand can only help. If there is nothing specific that you have to deal with, then just keep yourself informed of what is going on in your neighbourhood.

SUNDAY, 18TH APRIL
Moon conjunct Venus
If you are asked to join in any kind of group activity today, then do so because you will get much more out of this than you had bargained for. You will make new friends and be filled with new and exciting ideas. It is possible that you will begin to realize that someone whom you had, hitherto, considered to be nothing more than a friend is rapidly turning into someone who is special to you.

LEO

MONDAY, 19TH APRIL
Mars opposite Saturn
This is not the day in which to take on those who are in positions of power or authority over you. It would be better to let sleeping bosses lie or to leave things as they are. If you try to change the *status quo* in any way, you will come a cropper. It may be that you are right in your thinking, but others will simply not be ready to see things the way that you do now.

TUESDAY, 20TH APRIL
Sun into Taurus
The Sun moves decisively into your horoscopic area of ambition from today bringing in a month when your worldly progress will achieve absolute priority. You need to feel that what you are doing is worthwhile and has more meaning than simply paying the bills. You may feel the urge to change you career, to make a long-term commitment to a worthwhile cause, or simply to demand recognition for past efforts. However this ambitious phase manifests, you can be sure that your prospects are considerably boosted from now on.

WEDNESDAY, 21ST APRIL
Venus opposite Pluto
One of your hopes will now be seen as being mistaken. However the news isn't all bad since another avenue for your talents will be revealed to you. Keep your friends and your lovers apart, because they will either hate each other or they may run off with each other, leaving you standing alone!

THURSDAY, 22ND APRIL
Mercury sextile Neptune
Common sense is a rare commodity today since you are too busy basking in an aura of romantic dreams and fantasies. If your lover is far away, then you'll have a strong urge to make contact now.

FRIDAY, 23RD APRIL
Jupiter sextile Uranus
The combination of Jupiter and Uranus inspires optimism today. This is a good time for travel, especially in company with a loved one. A suggestion for a trip may come out of the blue and be accepted at once!

SATURDAY, 24TH APRIL
Sun opposite Mars
Being such a hard worker, you realize how difficult it can be to maintain the cash

for your lifestyle, so it will be easy to become angered by the spendthrift attitude of some people around you today. You may find that so-called friends are all too willing to spend your money while retaining their own by claiming they are broke. Don't stand for any nonsense now. Put your foot down and refuse to supplement extravagance.

SUNDAY, 25TH APRIL
Moon trine Saturn

There seems to be a real window of opportunity opening for you now. A person in a position of authority may give you just the kind of advice you need and he or she could do something really practical to help your cause now. If you deal with the public in any way or if you are involved in helping or advising people, you should have considerable success in your endeavours now.

MONDAY, 26TH APRIL
Mercury trine Pluto

If you have been involved in any kind of creative enterprise, it looks as though it is set to take off like a rocket today. You will soon have just the opportunity you need to get your ideas off the ground and to really make something of them.

TUESDAY, 27TH APRIL
Sun conjunct Saturn

This should be a turning-point day in which you reach a particular objective that you have had your sights set on. You may want to shine in a social setting or to achieve something solid in business, and the events of today will help you do either one of these things. You will have to pay attention to details and to make sure that you have crossed all the t's and dotted all the i's before you can say that your work is finished for the day.

WEDNESDAY, 28TH APRIL
Moon opposite Mercury

Your wonderfully logical, practical and sensible brain is on strike today. You will just not be able to think straight or to come up with a sensible answer to anything today, so don't try. Leave any important decisions until the stars have moved into a better position for the time being. It is not a good day to sign anything important either.

THURSDAY, 29TH APRIL
Mercury sextile Uranus

Your mind is working at full pelt today and you are absolutely full of original ideas. These are bound to impress others and maybe even surprise those who love you.

LEO

FRIDAY, 30TH APRIL
Full Moon

The Full Moon today focuses firmly on family and domestic issues. Perhaps this is the time for some straight talking because this is the best opportunity you'll get to put an end to home-based or emotional problems. In some ways it's time to put your cards on the table, yet equally to give credit and take some share of blame in family affairs. Apart from such personal concerns it's time to speak to someone in authority about your ambitions.

May at a Glance

LOVE	❤				
WORK	★	★	★	★	★
MONEY	£	£	£		
HEALTH	✚	✚			
LUCK	U	U			

SATURDAY, 1ST MAY
Mercury conjunct Jupiter

The planet-given clarity of mind has given you renewed confidence, boosting your optimism no end. This is a good time to send off cards to friends in distant parts of the world. Show that those who are far away are still in your thoughts.

SUNDAY, 2ND MAY
Moon sextile Neptune

A sudden declaration of love is not unlikely today. The emotions are very close to the surface and no matter how you repress them, they are still likely to bubble over into many areas of your life. Apart from the physical aspect of this, a deep spiritual attachment and need will be felt.

MONDAY, 3RD MAY
Moon sextile Uranus

If you are bored and lonely, then ring up a couple of your friends, because they are probably in much the same mood as yourself. If you all meet and do something on an impromptu basis, you will probably end up having the time of your lives. A friend could introduce you to a new face who may be destined to become an important part of your future.

TUESDAY, 4TH MAY
Moon opposite Venus

Your energy level is low at the moment, so don't set yourself a list of tiresome tasks. Just go through the motions while at work. Plan an evening of resting on the sofa, watching your favourite video or chatting idly to your lover. Don't put any demands upon yourself today, get a 'take-away' dinner (a 'carry-out' to all our American readers!), and read the papers until you doze off.

WEDNESDAY, 5TH MAY
Mars into Libra

Mars marches into your communications house today, so being direct, not to say forceful in speech will be a feature of the next few weeks. If you've got something to say, then there's no power in heaven or earth that's going to prevent you from saying it! If talking to a friend or relative has been like walking on eggshells, you'll make it clear that you aren't going to pussyfoot around sensitive topics any more! Be prepared for some heated words to clear the air!

THURSDAY, 6TH MAY
Moon square Jupiter

Your problem now is knowing when to quit while you're ahead. It might have done to push your luck recently but today caution should be your watchword. We know that your hopes have been lifted but you also have to keep your feet on the ground. In a work or health situation, listen to the words of a friend who has your welfare at heart.

FRIDAY, 7TH MAY
Neptune retrograde

No matter how hard you try, you won't be able to make sense of your partner's illogical attitudes today. It's all the fault of Neptune who turns retrograde, thus complicating and confusing a close partnership. I hope that you are an organized type because you'll soon have to take a loved one or business partner in hand. Keep a close watch on the finances because someone you rely on isn't being very rational, either about emotions or with cash.

SATURDAY, 8TH MAY
Mercury into Taurus

There's a certain flexibility entering your career structure as indicated by the presence of Mercury in your Solar area of ambition from today. You can now turn your acute mind to all sorts of career problems and solve them to everyone's satisfaction, and your own personal advantage. Your powers of persuasion will be heightened from now on, ensuring that you charm bosses and employers to get your own way. Those seeking work should attend interviews because their personality will shine.

SUNDAY, 9TH MAY
Mercury sextile Venus

A private inspiration will be a source of comfort to you today. In career affairs your vision of what is possible may not be appreciated by those around you, but you know it to be true. Keep faith, because you will achieve it in the end.

MONDAY, 10TH MAY
Moon square Pluto

Something may go strangely wrong with your sex life today. It may be one of those occasions when either you or your partner simply can't turn it on. Alternatively, you may both be trying too hard to impress each other, wearing yourselves out without really enjoying the experience. Relax back for a while and try not to make such a production of lovemaking. Listen to some music together, share a glass of wine and then let everything take its course – if it wants to.

TUESDAY, 11TH MAY
Mercury square Neptune

The groundless fears of someone close could make you equally as jittery if you allow your anxieties to get the better of you. If you think logically, many of the problems that present themselves today will prove to be totally false.

WEDNESDAY, 12TH MAY
Moon trine Pluto

A sudden infatuation could take you by surprise today. But you must ask yourself whether a new person in your life is making you feel this way or is it just a case of them seeming to be more sophisticated, elegant and cosmopolitan than they actually are. Look beneath the surface before you commit yourself to a romantic course.

THURSDAY, 13TH MAY
Mercury conjunct Saturn

A problem seems to be solving itself for you now. The right person with the right ideas will help you to push forward and to achieve your objectives. If you speak out to others, you will be listened to, and other people may come up with ideas and systems that help you to get where you want to be. An older person or one who is in a position of responsibility will help you now.

FRIDAY, 14TH MAY
Moon sextile Venus

There is an element of skulduggery going on at your place of work today, so don't make any major decisions or take much in the way of action until you know the strength of this. Away from work, the atmosphere is peaceful and charming and you can enjoy the company of friends, family and lovers in perfect harmony. Enjoy this oasis of pleasantness while it lasts because days like this are rare.

SATURDAY, 15TH MAY
New Moon

The New Moon today shows the great heights that you could possibly attain. The message is that there's nothing to fear except fear itself. Reach for the stars and you've got it made. Your career should begin to blossom now and you can achieve the kind of respect and status that you are looking for over the next month or so.

SUNDAY, 16TH MAY
Venus sextile Saturn

A woman could put a good word in for you at your place of work or she may help you by letting you know what is about to happen. This is a good time to make long-term plans of all kinds. If you look around your neighbourhood now, you will find plenty of opportunities to improve your work prospects, you social standing or anything else that makes you feel happy and successful. It is also a good time to start any kind of writing project.

MONDAY, 17TH MAY
Mercury square Uranus

'You can't please all of the people all of the time', That's the astral message for the day. A lot of pressure will be piled on today, both in a relationship setting and at work. You can't be expected to do everything, so why try? However, explaining this will be difficult, to say the least.

TUESDAY, 18TH MAY
Moon sextile Saturn

You feel the need for some solitude today. Future planning in the career sense is at the forefront of your mind, so take the phone off the hook, lock the door and have a good hard think.

LEO

WEDNESDAY, 19TH MAY
Moon square Jupiter
You're delving into your own private world again today. The power of your imagination is very strong and you can see things not as they are, but as they should be in an ideal world. You may review your life and realize how much you have learned as well as how much you've gained in the material sense.

THURSDAY, 20TH MAY
Moon opposite Neptune
Who is fooling whom? That's the question as the Moon moves into opposition with the confusing planet Neptune. If you are playing emotional games with someone close, then stop at once. One or other, possibly both, will get hurt.

FRIDAY, 21ST MAY
Sun into Gemini
As the Sun makes its yearly entrance into your eleventh Solar house, you can be sure that friends and acquaintances are going to have a powerful influence on your prospects. The Sun's harmonious angle to your own sign gives an optimism and vitality to your outgoing nature. Social life will increase in importance over the next month. You'll be a popular and much sought-after person. Obstacles that have irritated you will now be swept away.

SATURDAY, 22ND MAY
Uranus retrograde
If your relationships have become stifling, then take your cue from the eccentric planet Uranus, and take a more independent stance starting today. Many of your problems stem from the fact that a too close association can end up as a suffocating force in life. You both need a little breathing space, so don't think you are being disloyal just because you want to do something on your own.

SUNDAY, 23RD MAY
Mercury into Gemini
The swift-moving planet Mercury enters your eleventh Solar house today and gives a remarkable uplift to your social prospects. During the next few weeks you'll find yourself at the centre point of friendly interactions. People will seek you out for the pleasure of your company. It's also a good time to get in contact with distant friends and those you haven't seen for a while. The only fly in the ointment is that you shouldn't expect a small phone bill.

LEO

MONDAY, 24TH MAY
Moon trine Mercury

You won't be able to complain of being kept in the dark today because there seem to be messages, letters, phone calls and faxes coming at you from all directions. You may need to attend to paperwork or to details of some kind at your place of work. Try to keep all these bits of paper together in one place (especially those that relate to money), because they may get lost.

TUESDAY, 25TH MAY
Sun trine Neptune

Your hopes and wishes are a step nearer to fulfilment as the Sun makes an excellent contact with Neptune today. You have the backing of your lover and your friends now, and will gain an inner certainty that your dreams can come true. Believing is half the battle!

WEDNESDAY, 26TH MAY
Sun conjunct Mercury

The conjunction of the Sun and Mercury makes this one of the most exciting days of the year. Your mentality is on top from and communications of all kinds will work to your benefit. You can't let others make all the running now, get out and about, circulate. You'll find that friends, colleagues and supporters will all help you make your dreams come true. You have the heaven-sent ability to be in the right place at the right time, and, more importantly, to say the right things!

THURSDAY, 27TH MAY
Moon square Neptune

You are extremely sensitive to criticism today from those close to you. It's just one of those times when you see an implication in nearly everything that's said or done. Remember that not everything is directed at you, so don't over-react.

FRIDAY, 28TH MAY
Moon square Uranus

The family is fraught with tension today as a relative seems set on stirring up old problems that have long since been buried. You shouldn't rise to the bait and should avoid confrontations that you couldn't possibly win!

SATURDAY, 29TH MAY
Mars opposite Jupiter

Stop, think and decide whether you really need to make that journey today. If you can put off any kind of travel for the next few days, then you should do so.

If you need to get in touch with anybody now, be diplomatic and keep your temper in check.

SUNDAY, 30TH MAY
Full Moon

Your creative soul and romantic yearnings come under the influence of today's Full Moon, so it's time to take stock of those things in your life that no longer give any emotional satisfaction. Children and younger people may need a word or two of advice now and the love lives of all around you will become the centre of interest. You're own romantic prospects may see an upturn too.

MONDAY, 31ST MAY
Venus square Mars

Your private life is the area of concern today. The harsh aspect between Venus and Mars highlights a secret love in your life, so clandestine relationships may be revealed for what they are if you aren't careful. A misguided word or deed could alert the world to a passion that you'd rather keep to yourself.

June at a Glance

LOVE	❤	❤	❤	❤	
WORK	★	★	★	★	★
MONEY	£	£	£		
HEALTH	✪				
LUCK	∪	∪	∪	∪	∪

TUESDAY, 1ST JUNE
Venus square Jupiter

Though you're much in demand socially, you'll be in no mood to stick to one person or topic for very long today. Those two benefic planets, Venus and Jupiter, successfully increase your charm but also add a wicked element of flirtation and teasing. At least this will give you a very alluring and enigmatic aura. Foreigners or news from abroad will again be a feature of the day.

LEO

WEDNESDAY, 2ND JUNE
Sun opposite Pluto

There isn't much agreement on anything today. The Sun opposes Pluto bringing you into contact with argumentative people and stubborn acquaintances who refuse to see your point of view. Children too may push their luck and be rewarded with a scolding. There isn't much you can do to change another's entrenched prejudice so remove yourself from strife at the earliest opportunity.

THURSDAY, 3RD JUNE
Mars direct

If you have had some kind of physical problem with your arms, hands, shoulders or your upper spine, you could start to find a way of curing this now. You may visit an osteopath or you may go in for some other kind of physical therapy in order to get this straightened out. There may be something new for you to learn or a new process for you to get to grips with but the next few weeks will bring about a turning point in all of this too.

FRIDAY, 4TH JUNE
Mercury trine Mars

It's a day of good news, helpful friends and pleasant journeys. The mingled influences of Mercury and Mars will lift your spirits and put you in an extremely sociable mood. Make the most of it!

SATURDAY, 5TH JUNE
Venus into Leo

The luxury-loving planet, Venus, is suggesting that this is a great time to spoil yourself and also to enjoy yourself. So treat yourself to something nice and new that is for you alone. A new outfit would be a good idea or a few nice-smelling toiletries. Throw a party for your favourite friends and don't look the other way if someone seems to be fancying you.

SUNDAY, 6TH JUNE
Moon square Pluto

You're in a passionate frame of mind, and your thoughts will stray back to memories of intimate moments again and again. It's not just memories either, for you'll be busy working out a way to make your sensual fantasies come true. If by chance your attention is drawn back to the real world, you'll find that a youngster is in a particularly awkward and obstructive mood.

LEO

MONDAY, 7TH JUNE
Mercury into Cancer

You'll find yourself in a more introspective mood for a few weeks because Mercury, planet of the mind, enters the most secret and inward-looking portion of your horoscope from today. This is the start of a period when you'll want to understand the inner being, your own desires and motivations. Too much hectic life will prove a distraction now so go by instinct and seek out solitude when you feel like it.

TUESDAY, 8TH JUNE
Sun trine Uranus

A friend of a friend could give you a compliment out of the blue which will do much to boost your self-esteem and convince you that what you are doing is right! Many of your hopes will now show signs of fruition.

WEDNESDAY, 9TH JUNE
Moon sextile Uranus

Whatever you start doing today, you'll end up doing something else. The Lunar aspect to Uranus gives you a wandering mind, and where the mind goes the feet will soon follow. Routine tasks hold no appeal now since you can think of a million and one things that you'd rather be doing. Give in to the impulse if you possibly can, because anyone who expects you to knuckle down today is living in dreamland.

THURSDAY, 10TH JUNE
Venus opposite Neptune

There is no doubt about it, you don't know what to expect from lovers, partners or working associates these days. This is nothing new; you have been experiencing ups and downs in your love life for quite a few years and it may be a few more yet before this area of your life is completely straightforward once again.

FRIDAY, 11TH JUNE
Moon square Uranus

You may have to rush away from work in order to sort out something for your partner. Alternatively, you may have to leave your partner to get on with things at home while you rush round to your place of work. It is hard to be competent and efficient in all areas of life and today's rather unexpected events will show you that you only have one pair of hands.

LEO

SATURDAY, 12TH JUNE
Moon trine Neptune

Today should be a social extravaganza for you and for someone special in your life. Don't be a pair of wallflowers, get out into the social whirl and have a ball!

SUNDAY, 13TH JUNE
New Moon

There's no doubt that issues surrounding friendship and trust are very important now. The New Moon in your horoscopic area of social activities ensures that encounters with interesting people will yield new and enduring friendships. Though your mood has tended to vary between optimism and despair recently, the New Moon can't fail to increase your confidence and vitality.

MONDAY, 14TH JUNE
Venus trine Pluto

Take your lover out somewhere nice today. Eat, drink and be very, very merry. There may be something to celebrate now, but even if there isn't try celebrating just for the hell of it.

TUESDAY, 15TH JUNE
Mercury sextile Saturn

Good news from bosses and authority figures is to be expected today. You may dread encounters with people of importance, but the events of the day should prove that they are well disposed towards you, and are willing to say so in no uncertain terms.

WEDNESDAY, 16TH JUNE
Sun trine Mars

You are in an exceptionally energetic frame of mind now and you will want to get up and get on with things today. Friends may take you out to unusual places or you could find yourself going somewhere new and exciting. Romance could be in the air but, if so, you will find your new lover better to talk to than to make love to today. You are in the mood for talking and listening to others now.

THURSDAY, 17TH JUNE
Moon opposite Uranus

You may have planned the best possible day for yourself and your lover, only to find that Murphy's Law is in operation and nothing works out the way you had hoped. He or she may be around, but not in the mood to be pleasant or, alternatively, you may be too busy yourself to have much time to spare for social activities.

FRIDAY, 18TH JUNE
Moon trine Jupiter

With the added encouragement of Jupiter in your house of adventure and travel, the Moon urges movement in your life. This is not a day to sit at home knitting. Get out and about, meet people, go sightseeing. In short, anything that gives a new experience is favoured now. If you don't feel that you can just take off, then open a good book or watch an interesting documentary. The mind needs some expansion so give it the chance.

SATURDAY, 19TH JUNE
Venus square Saturn

If you are female, you could find this an obstacle to your advancement today. You may have to make the old familiar choice between a child who has an unscheduled day off school or away from the child-minder and your job. If you are a man, a woman may place pitfalls in your path in some way today.

SUNDAY, 20TH JUNE
Sun sextile Jupiter

Social life and celebrations should be the centre of attraction. It doesn't matter if you have to travel some distance to meet up with your friends because the journey will be worth it. You may even see another, fascinating side to someone you thought you knew well. A profound expression of wisdom will renew your interest.

MONDAY, 21ST JUNE
Sun into Cancer

The Sun moves into your house of secrets and psychology today making you very aware of your own inner world of dreams and imagination. For the next month you'll be very aware of the hurdles that face you, and all those things that tend to restrict your freedom; however your imagination and almost psychic insight will provide the necessary clues to overcome these obstacles. Issues of privacy are very important for the next few weeks.

TUESDAY, 22ND JUNE
Venus opposite Uranus

An apparently selfish attitude on your part will receive the most vehement opposition today. You could be putting your foot down too over the thoughtless actions of a partner.

LEO

WEDNESDAY, 23RD JUNE
Mercury square Mars

You may need to put on a show of bravado in order to prevent someone from undermining your position or stealing your thunder. This is all well and good, as long as you don't go over the top and lose all sense of proportion. You must also avoid acting recklessly or speaking without thinking of the effect of your words upon others and it would be a good idea to try to keep your temper too, if you can.

THURSDAY, 24TH JUNE
Moon opposite Saturn

Your parents could cause you some worry today and if you haven't got parents of your own, there could be worry and difficulties in connection with older people in your circle. They may be ill and needing help or they may be tiresome and demanding for no particular reason at all. You will have to work out whether you spend the day running around these people or whether you leave them to get on with things by themselves.

FRIDAY, 25TH JUNE
Mercury square Jupiter

The harsh aspect between Mercury and Jupiter casts the often uncomfortable light of reality into the darkest recesses of your imagination. Unreal dreams will be ruthlessly set aside as you get a much needed dose of common sense. This needn't be depressing at all, it just keeps your feet on the ground. The only danger to watch for is that you'll tend to be caught out if you lie or exaggerate.

SATURDAY, 26TH JUNE
Mercury into Leo

The movement of Mercury into your own sign signals the start of a period of much clearer thinking for you. You will know where you want to go and what you want to do from now on. It will be quite easy for you to influence others with the brilliance of your ideas and you will also be able to project just the right image. Guard against trying to crowd too much into one day today.

SUNDAY, 27TH JUNE
Moon trine Venus

Your mind will be on romance today and fate may encourage you to expresses your feelings to your loved one. It is a good day to treat your partner to a small gift, a night out in his or her favourite restaurant, to some theatre tickets or any other treat that you both would appreciate. You can forget the mundane world for a while today and concentrate on the fun side of life for once.

MONDAY, 28TH JUNE

Jupiter into Taurus

You are about to start a new phase which will be with you for the next year or so. This will enhance your job prospects and allow you to make the kind of money that you need. Your status out in the world will increase and you will become quite well known in your particular field of work. You may travel in search of work or start to spread your net wider in some way.

TUESDAY, 29TH JUNE

Moon trine Saturn

You should be in a businesslike mood today. The pressure's on and there'll be little opportunity for frivolity. At least all this hard work will pay off in the end because you'll be determined to win through to enjoy the fruits of your labours.

WEDNESDAY, 30TH JUNE

Mercury opposite Neptune

Tread carefully in relationship matters because you are likely to be misunderstood today. Words get garbled now, so avoid leaving messages that are open to misinterpretation and be ultra-clear when talking with a loved one.

July at a Glance

LOVE	❤	❤	❤	❤	
WORK	★	★	★	★	★
MONEY	£	£	£		
HEALTH	✪	✪	✪	✪	✪
LUCK	U				

THURSDAY, 1ST JULY

Moon sextile Pluto

You haven't got much time for small talk today because you are at the mercy of some deep emotions which you'll want to express to someone who means the world to you. For many this will be an ardent declaration of love. For others a renewal of vows made long ago. Feelings shown now could change your life.

LEO

FRIDAY, 2ND JULY
Moon opposite Venus

Your loved ones may be in a tetchy mood today, so steer clear of domestic disputes and try to get your lover and the kids to relax. Snuggle up in front of the fire, toast a few crumpets and open a bottle of something nice and warming. Get a pack of cards out or try your hands at a bit of Scrabble. This way, you will keep the domestic harmony going whilst avoiding getting cold and wet at the same time!

SATURDAY, 3RD JULY
Moon trine Mars

Money affairs are highlighted today with words of advice heading in your direction. Now if you are wise you'll listen carefully and give all suggestions regarding savings and investment the thought they deserve. You won't get far if you decide that you know best early on, and refuse to budge from your position. There are some valuable tips to be gleaned from any conversation today.

SUNDAY, 4TH JULY
Mars opposite Jupiter

Concentrate on getting your act together at home and at work now because, although things may be a bit quiet today, they will soon take off once again at a rate of knots. Keep your eye firmly on your goals and aspirations because you will rarely get better opportunities for advancement. Romance will come as a result of being in the public eye, so don't sit at home hiding behind closed doors.

MONDAY, 5TH JULY
Mars into Scorpio

That highly energetic planet, Mars, moves into your Solar fourth house today and it will stay there for the next few weeks. This will place quite a strong emphasis on the domestic area of your life, and it will be particularly favourable for those of you who are considering a move of house or of making fairly major changes to the one you are in now. It also brings an emphasis on family life and on nostalgia or of looking backwards for any other reason.

TUESDAY, 6TH JULY
Moon square Sun

There's a touch of oversensitivity about you today. We know you can usually brazen out unpleasant encounters, but just at the moment you'd far rather completely avoid awkward situations and people. Actually this is a good thing at the moment, so don't try to force yourself into any actions that you aren't completely happy with. Being assertive could hurt your interests just now.

LEO

WEDNESDAY, 7TH JULY
Moon trine Venus

You could have a rather nice day in company with in-laws or some other relative of your partner's today. A woman who is vaguely attached to you in this kind of way will turn out to be amusing and interesting company. This person could help you work out how best to go about decorating or changing part of your home or, if you need some help from an experienced cook, she could be the one to come up with the right recipe.

THURSDAY, 8TH JULY
Mercury trine Pluto

You will find a way of transforming something that is worn out or basically useless into something that can be used in a completely different way today. Creative thinking will be needed now.

FRIDAY, 9TH JULY
Moon square Venus

Venus's residence in your sign should be extremely helpful to you, and so it will be, but today there is a slight hiccup in all this. Women may be irritating to deal with, and someone may try to run you down either in front of your face or behind your back. This could be quite serious because it could temporarily block your progress in at least one important area of your life.

SATURDAY, 10TH JULY
Moon sextile Mercury

Prepare yourself for a party. It may not be planned but the Lunar aspect to Mercury ensures that an impromptu affair has all the makings of a splendid time. Forget your duties for now, and accept any invitation that comes your way without a second thought. On the other hand, you may find your home invaded by friends determined on a good time.

SUNDAY, 11TH JULY
Mars square Neptune

Passions run high today, though not necessarily in the wisest direction. You are prone to sudden infatuation and could simply lose your head over the object of your desire. You may find that you are more keen on romance than your partner!

MONDAY, 12TH JULY
Mercury retrograde

Confusion reigns today due to the fact that Mercury is moving backwards in your sign. Your usual logical and incisive mind may be filled with cotton wool and unable to act with its 'Spock-like' efficiency. If you are asked to guide the starship *Enterprise* today, you should refuse, because you would lose it for good somewhere in the outer reaches of the galaxy.

TUESDAY, 13TH JULY
New Moon

The world of romance is especially attractive on a day when your dreams and fantasies take over your life. The New Moon points the way to new emotional experiences in the future, but you mustn't cling to the past because of misplaced loyalty or guilt. Some people are leaving your life, but if you were honest you'd admit that they're no real loss. Follow your instincts now and your dreams may well come true.

WEDNESDAY, 14TH JULY
Moon conjunct Mercury

You are likely to be the starring act today wherever you happen to be. At work, your ideas will beam out far ahead of those of others and at home, your scintillating wit will impress your family and friends. You will be so sharp that you are in danger of cutting yourself on your own tongue today!

THURSDAY, 15TH JULY
Venus trine Jupiter

It's an excellent day in both money matters and career affairs. The two benefic planets, Venus and Jupiter, enter a positive aspect today showering you with luck and sudden opportunity. A job offer or other increase in prestige isn't too far away. This will not only enhance your own vision of yourself but boost your cash flow considerably too.

FRIDAY, 16TH JULY
Mercury trine Pluto

Nothing could possibly get past your keen perceptions today. Mercury and Pluto give you clear vision and the ability to see through the most confusing situation. In affairs of the heart especially, this gives you an advantage.

SATURDAY, 17TH JULY
Void Moon

The Moon is 'void of course' today, so don't bother with anything important and don't start anything new now. Stick to your usual routines and don't change your lifestyle in any way.

LEO

SUNDAY, 18TH JULY
Saturn square Uranus
You seem to be under considerable stress at the moment. It is likely that you will tend to take out your irritations on the person whom you love best. Though this is not to be commended, it is understandable under these trying circumstances.

MONDAY, 19TH JULY
Moon trine Uranus
Your mood is strangely independent and, fortunately for you, others will respect your need to make up your own mind about certain matters. Although there is a great deal going on in your circle, you seem to be able to maintain a strangely detached view of it all. Others may consider you to be slightly lofty or strangely idealist in your outlook.

TUESDAY, 20TH JULY
Moon square Sun
Other people are amazingly keen to remind you of things that you haven't done or jobs that you haven't finished and their bossy and interfering attitude is likely to drive you to distraction today. Just get on with what you have to do and tell your nagging friend or relative to get lost!

WEDNESDAY, 21ST JULY
Jupiter square Neptune
They say that a job worth doing is worth doing well; unfortunately you don't want to do it at all! The negative rays of Jupiter and Neptune urge you to rely solely upon luck, but this will get you nowhere. A more businesslike attitude is needed.

THURSDAY, 22ND JULY
Mercury square Mars
There seems to be a certain amount of pressure being placed upon you from the domestic area. This may manifest itself in the form of a practical problem in the home or to do with your home. If you have a small business, there could be something wrong there. Feelings may be running high all around you, and your own nerves seem to be rather stretched by all these problems.

FRIDAY, 23RD JULY
Sun into Leo
The Sun moves into your own sign today bringing with it a lifting of your spirits and a gaining of confidence all round. Your birthday will soon be here and we hope that it will be a good one for you. You may see more of your family than is

usual now and there should be some socializing and partying to look forward too. Music belongs to the realm of the Sun, so treat yourself to a musical treat soon.

SATURDAY, 24TH JULY
Moon sextile Uranus

If you have been coping with everything on your own recently, you will be delighted to find that this should no longer be the case. Your partner may have been too busy to pay you much attention lately, but now he or she will have more time to devote to you and more inclination to listen to your problems. Friends will be on hand to help you out today, and to give you both the listening ear and the advice that you most need.

SUNDAY, 25TH JULY
Mercury square Jupiter

As one who is constantly urging positive thinking, it comes hard to say that optimism is a very good thing as long as it isn't taken too far. Today's stressful aspect between Mercury and Jupiter is a case in point. Though your view of the career picture is extremely promising, aren't you relying a just a little too much on luck? Has your balanced perspective been replaced by wishful thinking? Try to keep your feet on the ground today.

MONDAY, 26TH JULY
Sun opposite Neptune

Relationships are dodgy ground today. The Solar opposition to Neptune shows that one or other partner will be living in a fantasy world and being their own worst enemy. When an attempt is made to point this out, a hostile reaction is to be expected. Play it cool, and allow this influence to pass.

TUESDAY, 27TH JULY
Sun square Jupiter

You will be propelled back into reality with a jolt. The demands placed on you now are very trying since you can't make any sense of the tasks you are asked to complete or the attitudes of those who set them. You may feel that your luck has deserted you, but that's not the case for you're being taught a valuable lesson, and it's up to you to see it.

WEDNESDAY, 28TH JULY
Full Moon eclipse

Today's eclipse casts a shadow of doubt over a close relationship. Problems that have been simmering under the surface will now come out and have to be faced.

It's no good shying away from serious issues because this can be a make-or-break time.

THURSDAY, 29TH JULY
Moon square Saturn

There may be something of a conflict between the interests of your partner and the interests of your employer. For example, your lover may want to move to another area where there would be more opportunities for his or her advancement and this may not be the right thing for you. This is simply one example, but it shows the kind of dilemma that you may have to face now.

FRIDAY, 30TH JULY
Sun trine Pluto

You may be obsessive, but this time your drive and ambition will have a good outcome. The Sun's aspect to intense Pluto enhances your creative talents and makes you a most magnetic and attractive character. Romantically, you will be extremely seductive and passionate.

SATURDAY, 31ST JULY
Mercury into Cancer retrograde

Mercury re-enters the most private and secluded area of your horoscope today showing that some time spent away from the mad rush of modern life would be a good idea. Take a break and do some thinking instead of rushing around.

August at a Glance

LOVE	❤	❤	❤		
WORK	★	★	★	★	
MONEY	£	£	£		
HEALTH	✚	✚	✚	✚	
LUCK	⛄	⛄	⛄	⛄	⛄

SUNDAY, 1ST AUGUST
Moon trine Mercury

You may look quite deeply into some really strange and unusual aspects of life today. You may be drawn into a discussion of the paranormal and it is even possible that you yourself could have a truly unforgettable experience. You may witness something really strange, such as levitation or ectoplasm. On the other hand, you may not see or do anything out of the ordinary but you could be intrigued by a book or a film which explores the unknown.

MONDAY, 2ND AUGUST
Moon trine Sun

The self-belief is restored and you'll relish some tough mental challenges. Though those whose eyes are set on foreign climes again get a boost to your travel fortunes. In fact, anything that expands mental horizons is favoured. All should go well on such an auspicious day.

TUESDAY, 3RD AUGUST
Venus trine Jupiter

It's bound to be a lucky day when Venus and Jupiter aspect each other. In your case maximum good fortune will occur in the career area, or indeed in any sphere which involves your aims and aspirations. Financial profit is probable too.

WEDNESDAY, 4TH AUGUST
Moon trine Venus

Attend to practical matters today and deal with anything to do with money now. If you talk to your bank manager about finances for a business idea, you will get some really useful advice and most probably all the help you require to go along with this. If you need to save up for some kind of future event or a future project, then set this in motion soon.

THURSDAY, 5TH AUGUST
Moon conjunct Saturn

You will have to get down to some hard work and some serious attention to detail today because Saturn, the task-master of the zodiac, is chasing your tail. Your boss may want a long and complicated job done by the end of the day and you may have to stay on in order to get it done. You may have a lot to do in the home and you could be late to bed tonight, owing to having stayed up late in order to get through it all.

FRIDAY, 6TH AUGUST
Mercury direct

Mercury returns to direct motion from today and that should put a stop to all the setbacks and disappointments that have bedevilled your career for the last few weeks. Suddenly, plans you'd put on the back burner are important again. Your path towards your aims will be much smoother than you expect. An ongoing dialogue with an employer or manager will be beneficial to your career prospects.

SATURDAY, 7TH AUGUST
Sun square Mars

You are in danger of silly accidents in the home today, so take things slowly and take care while doing jobs around the home. Make sure that the patio doors really are open before trying to walk through them and stack things on shelves properly, so that they don't end up falling down on you. You may find the family irritating now and it may be worth letting them see that their behaviour is getting on your nerves.

SUNDAY, 8TH AUGUST
Sun opposite Uranus

Your loved ones will behave in most peculiar ways today, doing the exact opposite of what you expect from them. You yourself could feel in a rebellious frame of mind as well. If you feel that your lover is behaving in a tyrannical or an inconsiderate manner, start to put your foot down now. Alternatively, you could leave your partner to get on with his or her life for a while, temporarily busying yourself with something else.

MONDAY, 9TH AUGUST
Moon sextile Saturn

You'll be in a particularly studious mood for much of the day. The stars favour study conducted in an atmosphere of solitude and peace. In fact anything you have to do that requires concentration will go well.

TUESDAY, 10TH AUGUST
Sun square Saturn

Someone or something may try to stand in the way of your progress today and it will be hard to get around this particular problem. You may have to accept that this is one of those days when you cannot get very far. You may be in the frustrating situation of not being able to get on with your main task because someone keeps pulling you away from it in order to do something that they should have done themselves in the first place.

WEDNESDAY, 11TH AUGUST
New Moon eclipse

According to Nostradamus, this is Doomsday! Sasha and Jonathan are more optimistic since it seems to be a new start for you as the Solar eclipse occurs in your sign. Put the past behind you. Close the door on all those things that have held you back. Painful memories might not actually go away, but at least you can put them in the perspective of your life as it is now. And indeed, as it will be in the future. Be positive, optimistic and outgoing. It's up to you to choose your future agenda — if, that is, old Nostradamus is wrong!

THURSDAY, 12TH AUGUST
Mercury into Leo

It seems to be the time for major planetary movements for Mercury races into your own sign now, giving you not only an eloquent tongue, but the opportunity to express your ideas and inspirations clearly and persuasively. You have a busy period coming up with constant letters and phone calls bringing gossip, laughs and fascinating information your way.

FRIDAY, 13TH AUGUST
Mercury opposite Neptune

You may not be able to put your finger on the reason why, but someone close is acting in an odd and disconcerting manner. You might have a disagreement with a loved one only to find that your arguments become circular and get you nowhere!

SATURDAY, 14TH AUGUST
Mars opposite Saturn

The weight of the world lies heavily on your shoulders today. There seems to be so much to do, with so little time to accomplish it all. Don't ask too much of yourself because you aren't superhuman. Just do what you can and be satisfied with that.

SUNDAY, 15TH AUGUST
Venus retrograde

Venus returns to your sign for an all too brief visit today. This charming planet will add her energy to your already considerable charisma and make you extra effective in the romantic stakes. However, don't let a sudden upsurge of popularity go to your head!

MONDAY, 16TH AUGUST
Moon sextile Sun

Keep abreast of the news today because something that is happening in your locality could be just the thing that you most want and need. Letters and phone calls should bring excellent news, especially if they come from other members of the family.

TUESDAY, 17TH AUGUST
Mercury square Jupiter

An opportunity for advancement will not be as promising as it first appears. If attending an interview or other sort of performance test, then choose your words with care or you may find that you're talking yourself out of a job!

WEDNESDAY, 18TH AUGUST
Moon opposite Saturn

You seem to be in a phase where it is hard for you to reconcile matters related to home and work. Home life is probably trolling along fairly peacefully but work may be awkward in some way. It may be hard to balance the demands of your home and family with your work. For instance, your employers may want you to work uncongenial hours or to get to work at a time that is awkward from a family point of view.

THURSDAY, 19TH AUGUST
Pluto direct

Pluto turns to direct motion today in your Solar fifth house. This means that any problems that you may have had with children or young people will begin to get themselves sorted out now. A love affair that has been held up by lack of cash or by strange circumstances should start to go in the direction that you most want. In addition to this, any creative projects that you are involved with will now begin to move forward.

FRIDAY, 20TH AUGUST
Sun conjunct Venus

The conjunction of the Sun and Venus in your own sign is the perfect indicator of romance. Charismatic to a fault you can easily attract anyone who takes your fancy. For many, this is merely going to mean a pleasant flirtation. For others, this could be the start of a lasting romance. However it turns out, this is a most enjoyable period in which your personality will shine.

SATURDAY, 21ST AUGUST
Moon trine Venus

There's a gentle and loving influence today with a gentle line up of the Moon and Venus. This is a time to pour oil on troubled waters and put old differences and grips to rest once and for all. You'll find great peace in involving yourself in creative activities. Express your talents now and you'll find a deep tranquillity evolving in your soul.

LEO

SUNDAY, 22ND AUGUST
Moon trine Jupiter

After some of the pressures you've been under, careerwise and in terms of burning the candle at both ends, it's time you looked at the state your physique is getting into. The Moon's aspect to Jupiter points out the benefits of a new health regime. This is a good day to work out with some aerobics, or if that's too energetic, moderate your intake with a new diet. Look after yourself.

MONDAY, 23RD AUGUST
Sun into Virgo

Your financial prospects take an upturn from today as the Sun enters your house of money and possessions. The next month should see an improvement in your economic security. It may be that you need to lay plans to ensure maximum profit now. Don't expect any swift returns from investments but lay down a pattern for future growth. Sensible monetary decisions made now will pay off in a big way.

TUESDAY, 24TH AUGUST
Venus square Mars

Keep your mind on what you are doing in and around the home today. Mars is badly aspected and this could bring silly accidents while working around the place. It is a poor day for getting on with home improvements, decorating, dressmaking or fancy cooking. It would be better either to go out and get on with jobs elsewhere or simply to relax and forget the chores for once.

WEDNESDAY, 25TH AUGUST
Jupiter retrograde

You would be a fool if you thought that everything in your professional world was going to go without any hitches. Jupiter turns retrograde today ensuring that career affairs slow down and people in authority throw spanners into the works. However, that's not the only astral influence current now. Uranus makes a move into a new sign now, hinting that this is the start of a process wherein you question your whole direction and wonder what it is exactly that you want to achieve.

THURSDAY, 26TH AUGUST
Full Moon

The Full Moon brings to the surface intense feelings that you have buried away in some vault of memory. You'll be forced to look at yourself stripped bare of illusions now. That's not such a bad things because you'll realize that many of your hang-ups have been a total waste of time and should be ditched. You may have a financial worry coming to a head so today's Full Moon encourages you to take decisive action to sort it out once and for all.

FRIDAY, 27TH AUGUST
Mercury conjunct Venus

Your personality is shown off to its best advantage today. You are bound to win admirers not just because of your looks but also for your wit and perception. With all this going for you how can you fail – at anything?

SATURDAY, 28TH AUGUST
Sun trine Jupiter

There's a financial theme in your stars, but this time it's very promising indeed. The Sun makes a marvellous aspect to Jupiter now so if you were thinking of asking for a raise, bank loan or other sort of investment in your future then do it now. This combination of Solar influence and jovial fortune makes you a difficult person to refuse. This could just be the start of a period of affluence.

SUNDAY, 29TH AUGUST
Moon trine Pluto

It's a day for fun and pure self-indulgence. You could be celebrating something, and if that's so then why not treat yourself to something special. A night out with a special person could be just the tonic you need.

MONDAY, 30TH AUGUST
Saturn retrograde

Saturn turns to retrograde motion in your tenth Solar house of aims and ambitions. Over the next few weeks you will notice a slowing down of your progress. It may be harder than usual to get through what you need to and, if you are in business, you will go through a slow patch. If you work for someone, you may feel unappreciated. Everything will come out in the wash all right in the end but it may be a bit hard living through this phase while it lasts.

TUESDAY, 31ST AUGUST
Mercury into Virgo

All the planets seem to be restless just now since Mercury changes sign today. At least you can get your mind into gear concerning the state of your finances now. Tasks you've been putting off like cancelling useless standing orders, or ensuring you receive the most advantageous interest from your savings will be tackled with ease now.

LEO

September at a Glance

LOVE	❤	❤	❤	❤	❤
WORK	★	★			
MONEY	£	£	£	£	
HEALTH	✛	✛	✛		
LUCK	♘				

WEDNESDAY, 1ST SEPTEMBER
Moon square Venus

Though your working life isn't entirely conducive to your frame of mind, it wouldn't do to let your duties slide completely. There are lots of things to do, and though you can't really be bothered with boring tasks, you're going to have to knuckle down for today at least. Apparent goodwill from a boss or other authority figure may not live up to its promise so keep your nose to the grindstone.

THURSDAY, 2ND SEPTEMBER
Mars into Sagittarius

Mars moves into a very creative area of your chart now, so if there is a project that you would like to get started upon, Mars will give you the drive and energy with which to do it. This is a good day for any kind of sporting or energetic pursuit, so if you want to practise your skills or get ready for some kind of future competition, then get down to it today.

FRIDAY, 3RD SEPTEMBER
Mercury trine Jupiter

It'll be important for you to show exactly what you can do and what you are made of. In an interview situation the planetary combination of Mercury and Jupiter makes you an impressive contender. If you've an argument to put to those in authority, then this is the day and you're the person to win through.

SATURDAY, 4TH SEPTEMBER
Mercury square Pluto

Something is likely to come to light today and, while it is always a good idea to know what is going on, you may be less than charmed by what you hear. Someone may be jealous of your creative talent or your success, and this may come to light in a particularly unpleasant manner. On the other hand, this incident will show you who your true friends are.

SUNDAY, 5TH SEPTEMBER
Moon sextile Saturn

Achieving your ambitions can be a hard slog at times, yet forethought today will provide you with an excellent strategy for future action. You will find that a difficult job once accomplished will give an enormous sense of satisfaction.

MONDAY, 6TH SEPTEMBER
Mars sextile Neptune

Today's stars are marvellous for partnerships of all kinds, both business and those of a more personal nature. Mars and Neptune ensure that male influences will be more beneficial today than female. However, a strong understanding can now be built between almost any two people.

TUESDAY, 7TH SEPTEMBER
Moon opposite Uranus

The last person you expected to turn on you could do just that today. All personal relationships and even close working associations are extremely fraught just at the moment and you will have to make up your mind as to the best way to tackle these. It may be worth actually having a good row with somebody now, if only to show that you are not to be treated as a doormat.

WEDNESDAY, 8TH SEPTEMBER
Sun conjunct Mercury

This is an excellent day in which to pull off a really spectacular deal, so if you feel like wheeling and dealing in the big leagues, then do so today! Even if you are only looking around for something for yourself or your family, you should be able to find just what you want now. This is also a good time for buying or selling a vehicle, or for getting one put back in good working order.

THURSDAY, 9TH SEPTEMBER
New Moon

Today's New Moon shows that your financial affairs have reached a point where you have to make a decision. Do you carry on in the old and rather dreary ways of making and spending your cash or will you look at the realities and make sensible decisions? This isn't a time to retreat into dreamland, or to carry on with bad budgeting. Look at your monetary state carefully now.

LEO

FRIDAY, 10TH SEPTEMBER
Sun trine Saturn

This is a good day for putting long-term plans into action. If you have been looking for a way out of your present troubles, then, today, something could show you the best route to go for. A person in a position of responsibility or authority could be very helpful with both suggestions and also practical aid of some kind.

SATURDAY, 11TH SEPTEMBER
Venus direct

If you've attracted attention simply because you've given the impression of being cold and aloof recently, be prepared for even more of an impact as the thaw sets in and you suddenly become the most charming person around!

SUNDAY, 12TH SEPTEMBER
Moon sextile Venus

You're particularly charming and seductive today. You could use your wiles to get your own way in anything, as there are few with enough mental resistance to turn you down flat! You'll be at the centre of attraction. Affection will be shown to you and you'll be left in no doubt that all around you regard you with fondness and respect.

MONDAY, 13TH SEPTEMBER
Moon square Neptune

If you want any peace today, it would be better to go out. Your partner and other family members will be very demanding of your time and attention. Usually, this would not be such a problem, but you are in a rather dreamy frame of mind now, and can't put up with too much pressure.

TUESDAY, 14TH SEPTEMBER
Moon opposite Saturn

You are being asked to choose between your home life and your career, but you have no intention of sacrificing one for the sake of the other. Over the next few weeks, you will have to find a way to cope with both and, hard as this may be, an answer will be found. Women may find themselves facing demands from two different men; maybe a partner and a boss, a father and a son, or an employee and a family member.

WEDNESDAY, 15TH SEPTEMBER
Mars conjunct Pluto

Love, sex, obsessive feelings and a completely over-the-top way of living seems to be the order of the day today. You may be swept up in a maelstrom of feeling, becoming truly alive for the very first time in your life. On the other hand, there could be some kind of real creative success or a spectacular achievement of some kind to celebrate. Great times to live in.

THURSDAY, 16TH SEPTEMBER
Mercury into Libra

Your mind will be going full speed ahead over the next few weeks and you are bound to come up with some really great new ideas. You will be very busy with the phone ringing off its hook and letters falling into your letter box by the ton. You will find yourself acting as a temporary secretary for a while, even if the only person who makes use of your services is yourself.

FRIDAY, 17TH SEPTEMBER
Mercury trine Neptune

If you need to talk things over with your partner, have a go at this today. The chances are that he or she will be willing to talk and also to listen, but the planets are suggesting that what your other half would really enjoy is a good old-fashioned necking session. Perhaps you can combine both of these activities?

SATURDAY, 18TH SEPTEMBER
Moon square Mercury

You may feel slightly irritated today and it may be hard to get any sense out of anyone. You could be a bit under the weather and something unpleasant such as a cold or a visit to the dentist may spoil your day for you. Everything to do with work will be awkward and irritating and it will be hard to get new projects off the ground. Neighbours and colleagues may get on your nerves and the cat may do something nasty on your best carpet! All in all, a bit of a duff day.

SUNDAY, 19TH SEPTEMBER
Moon trine Saturn

If you are looking for a new job or seeking recognition or promotion in an existing one, today should fulfil your hopes. The Lunar aspect to Saturn shows that you will receive a reward from on high.

MONDAY, 20TH SEPTEMBER
Moon trine Sun

This should be a day of harmony since the Sun and Moon are in perfect agreement. Your emotions will be under control so there's little that could upset you or cause any panic. Routine will be important to you now so you can organize your time to achieve the maximum benefit. Work, health and money matters are all favoured.

TUESDAY, 21ST SEPTEMBER
Mercury sextile Pluto

If you take a look around your neighbourhood today, you are sure to be able to locate a bargain or two. You may have to negotiate a bit for what you want but that is part of the fun, isn't it?

WEDNESDAY, 22ND SEPTEMBER
Moon opposite Venus

The Moon's opposition to Venus shows you and a partner at loggerheads. Each party in this relationship will regard the other as being totally unreasonable at present and there's the danger of blowing minor disagreements into full-scale conflict. The secret of any lasting partnership is give and take, so bear that in mind when addressing the issues that separate you now.

THURSDAY, 23RD SEPTEMBER
Sun into Libra

Your curiosity will be massively stimulated from today as the Sun enters the area of learning and communication. Other people's business suddenly becomes your own now. That's not to say that you turn into a busybody overnight, it's just that many will turn to you for some guidance. Affairs in the lives of your brothers, sisters and neighbours have extra importance now. Short journeys too are well starred for one month.

FRIDAY, 24TH SEPTEMBER
Mars sextile Uranus

This is not going to be a boring day! Mars and Uranus ensure that there will be fireworks, yet these will not be of the destructive sort! In all affairs of the heart, passion rules!

SATURDAY, 25TH SEPTEMBER
Full Moon

You may have to face the fact that you cannot slope off to distant and romantic shores just now. This doesn't mean that you are forever confined to your home, just that you cannot get away right now. Your mood is not only escapist but also rebellious today! You won't want to have anything to do with people who restrict you or who remind you of your chores and duties but you simply won't be able to escape them.

LEO

SUNDAY, 26TH SEPTEMBER
Moon opposite Mercury

Watch your words today, because as quickly as you open your mouth, you'll manage to offend somebody. You may not mean to be sarcastic or indiscreet but for some reason your brain isn't tied into your speech centres at the moment. At the very least you'll be talking at cross-purposes with someone today. At worst, you'll turn a friend into an enemy by blurting out a private confidence that shouldn't be spoken.

MONDAY, 27TH SEPTEMBER
Moon square Neptune

Do as little as possible at work today. This is not a recipe for laziness, just an exercise in damage limitation. You are not functioning on top form anyway so mistakes are likely.

TUESDAY, 28TH SEPTEMBER
Moon conjunct Saturn

You are on the point of being rewarded for the work you have put in over the last few months. Life has been hard and to some extent it still is, but you are getting there and it is worth keeping on to the end of the road. There could well be a good opportunity for you to improve your position in your neighbourhood or your community now too.

WEDNESDAY, 29TH SEPTEMBER
Moon trine Neptune

The Moon contacts Neptune today making you very receptive to the thoughts and feelings of all around you. You will be sympathetic and of a charitable disposition, keen to alleviate any suffering that you can.

THURSDAY, 30TH SEPTEMBER
Moon trine Uranus

This is an excellent day for a party. If you haven't got an excuse, then make one up because you're in the mood for fun. The more the merrier that's your motto now, so invite some friends around for a gathering in your home. Single people may find a soulmate since you're determined to do some matchmaking.

October at a Glance

LOVE	♥	♥			
WORK	★				
MONEY	£	£	£	£	£
HEALTH	✪				
LUCK	♘	♘	♘		

FRIDAY, 1ST OCTOBER
Sun sextile Pluto

Don't let other people obscure the picture today. If there's something you have to say, or indeed something you have to find out, particularly in relation to affairs of the heart, make sure that everything is clear and above board.

SATURDAY, 2ND OCTOBER
Mercury sextile Venus

Your obvious charm is stimulated today as Venus makes a wonderful aspect to Mercury. There's a powerful attraction in the sound of your voice. You could persuade anyone that black was white, while your admirers are mesmerized by your velvet tones. A short journey could being you into contact with someone who catches your eye. Don't be shy, speak up – who knows where it could lead?

SUNDAY, 3RD OCTOBER
Moon square Mercury

We just knew all that talking was a mixed blessing. Your mind is racing so fast you can't help causing misunderstandings just now. You may also receive some wounding criticism, though you must admit that you're being a touch over-sensitive. If these hurtful words were actually meant to be constructive, then you could do worse than thinking hard about the issues they raise.

MONDAY, 4TH OCTOBER
Moon sextile Sun

This is a harmonious time when you can express the inner you and find warmth and understanding from those around you. You are charming and persuasive and will be showing your character off to the best advantage.

TUESDAY, 5TH OCTOBER
Mercury into Scorpio

The past exerts a powerful influence as Mercury enters the house of heritage. You'll find that things long forgotten will somehow re-enter your life over the next couple of weeks. An interest in your family heritage may develop, or possibly a new-found passion for antiques. Some good, meaningful conversations in the family will prove enlightening.

WEDNESDAY, 6TH OCTOBER
Sun trine Uranus

You and your partner are facing changes at the moment, but there is no reason for you to fear this because the signs are that these changes are welcome to you both. There may be more communication between yourselves and other members of the family now than you usually have. Friends will drop in, bringing interesting and exciting news of their own.

THURSDAY, 7TH OCTOBER
Venus into Virgo

Your financial state should experience a welcome boost for a few weeks as Venus, one of the planetary indicators of wealth, moves into your Solar house of possessions and economic security from today. You feel that you deserve a lifestyle full of luxury now and that'll be reflected in the good taste you express when making purchases for your home. Your sense of self-worth is boosted too which might indicate a renewed interest in high fashion.

FRIDAY, 8TH OCTOBER
Moon trine Neptune

A vague rumour will intrigue you today. You'll be determined to get to the bottom of it because you'll be convinced that there's no smoke without fire. You can't really take anything at face value today because there are mysterious undercurrents wherever you look. The answer to all puzzles lies with your intuition. Follow your hunches and they'll guide you more surely than conscious thought now.

SATURDAY, 9TH OCTOBER
New Moon

The New Moon shows a change in your way of thinking and in many ways you'll know that it's time to move on. Perhaps you'll find yourself in a new company, a new home or among a new circle of friends in the near future. Opinions are set to change as you are influenced by more stimulating people. Perhaps you'll consider taking up an educational course of some kind.

LEO

SUNDAY, 10TH OCTOBER
Venus trine Jupiter

The two lucky planets Venus and Jupiter combine forces today and will aid all your aims and aspirations in unexpected ways. Money too benefits from the influence of these planets so many can expect a more profitable career opportunity.

MONDAY, 11TH OCTOBER
Jupiter square Neptune

Neither work nor personal life looks particularly promising today. Neptune and Jupiter are at odds so there will be many demands made on you, vague problems to deal with and a general sense of boredom to contend with.

TUESDAY, 12TH OCTOBER
Void Moon

This is not a great day in which to decide anything or to start anything new. A void Moon suggests that there are no major planetary aspects being made, either between planets or involving the Sun or the Moon. This is a fairly unusual situation but it does happen from time to time and the only way to deal with it is to stick to your usual routines and do nothing special for a while.

WEDNESDAY, 13TH OCTOBER
Mercury square Uranus

Disturbing news could come like a bolt from the blue today. Perhaps an old skeleton is rattling in the cupboard or a family member makes a revelation that shakes you. The important thing is not to over-react. Whatever it is, it's not the end of the world.

THURSDAY, 14TH OCTOBER
Neptune direct

Today, that distant and very mysterious planet, Neptune, turns to direct motion. This will bring an end to any muddle and misunderstandings in connection with partnerships of all kinds. You will be able to get your personal relationships on a better footing and any working associations will be easier to handle. You will have more idea of what you want from these relationships and, therefore, it will be easier to tell others what you need from them.

FRIDAY, 15TH OCTOBER
Moon conjunct Mars

Your entire chart is energized by the Moon's conjunction with Mars today. This should inspire and activate all the romantic potentials in your life. The trouble is that you could get a little big-headed now, so you'll have to guard against being just a shade too forceful especially with a lover. Don't be too impulsive and domineering and you won't spoil the splendid day.

SATURDAY, 16TH OCTOBER
Mercury opposite Saturn

This is one of those days when there may be too many demands upon your time. Older relatives may be demanding or irritating today and they may try your patience or get on your nerves. There may be a clash between the disciplines and needs of your job and the needs and demands of your family. Whatever is claiming your attention today, there will be very little time for yourself.

SUNDAY, 17TH OCTOBER
Mars into Capricorn

The transit of Mars into your area of health and work shows that you must show that you have initiative and drive to make the most out of your prospects now. The energies of the fiery planet won't allow you to sink anonymously into a crowd. You'll be forced to stand out and make your mark on the professional world. In health affairs, the vitality of the planet must be good news. Rarely have you felt so alive and effective. You may find that some colleagues are distressed at this assertion of your personality and aims; unfortunately for them, they'll just have to put up with it!

MONDAY, 18TH OCTOBER
Venus square Pluto

The sudden arrival of a bill or another form of unexpected expense could cause you to regret your prodigality. Even so, this is a problem that can be solved even if you have to tighten your belt for a while to do it.

TUESDAY, 19TH OCTOBER
Moon square Saturn

The fairly grim Lunar aspect to Saturn inclines you to take a rather depressive view of life today. Both career worries and relationship disagreements could be blown out of proportion if you aren't careful.

WEDNESDAY, 20TH OCTOBER
Moon sextile Jupiter

Your fast thinking could save the day for someone in a position of authority today and this, in turn, could open a doorway of opportunity for you so be prepared to take advantage of bosses' goodwill. You could take a stride up the ladder of professional success now simply because you know how to keep a secret.

THURSDAY, 21ST OCTOBER
Moon opposite Venus

Don't be taken in by attractive offers or apparent bargains today, because you'll find that for every cent saved you'll pay a dollar in repair bills. Shoddy goods and glib promises are the main dangers so don't allow yourself to be gullible or to fall for attractive packaging. Equally, your desire to spend beyond your means should be curbed immediately.

FRIDAY, 22ND OCTOBER
Sun square Neptune

You may tend to look at your family, your lover and your close associates through rose-coloured glasses today, thinking that they are wonderful when in reality they are quite ordinary. You seem to be exceptionally willing to help out members of your family now, either in a practical manner or by handing over large sums of money. Make sure that this craziness doesn't go on for too long!

SATURDAY, 23RD OCTOBER
Sun into Scorpio

The home and family become your main interest over the next four weeks as the Sun moves into the most domestic area of your chart from today. Family feuds will now be resolved, and you'll find an increasing contentment in your own surroundings. A haven of peace will be restored in your home. This should also be a period of nostalgia when happy memories come flooding back.

SUNDAY, 24TH OCTOBER
Full Moon

Today's Full Moon shows that important decisions have to be made at a time of rapidly changing circumstances. News that arrives today could well be disturbing yet will prove to be a blessing in disguise in the long run. You may be considering a move of home, possibly to a distant location. Or even throwing in your present career to take up an educational course of some kind. People you meet while travelling will have important words to say.

MONDAY, 25TH OCTOBER
Venus trine Saturn

Apart from being the planet of love, Venus also is an indicator of financial well-being. Today's aspect of that planet with Saturn gives you the ability to put your cash affairs in order. You will be thrifty and sensible and able to build up your resources for the future.

TUESDAY, 26TH OCTOBER
Moon opposite Mercury

You may have to rush round to see one or other of your parents today. Alternatively, another older member of your circle could need your assistance now. The problem is that the messages that you are being given are a bit muddled and, when you actually look into the reality of the situation, it may be much better (or worse) than you first realized.

WEDNESDAY, 27TH OCTOBER
Moon opposite Pluto

You could show yourself in your worst possible light today if you aren't careful. If you don't feel that you are getting your own way, you'll be prepared to resort to underhanded tactics like emotional blackmail to make your other half feel guilty. You should be ashamed of yourself taking such unfair advantage of a perfectly innocent situation.

THURSDAY, 28TH OCTOBER
Mercury sextile Neptune

Words of love are music to your ears today. You are deeply sentimental and rather soft now, so the one thing you want is for someone close to tell you how much you mean to them. Creatively too, you are on top form. All artistic endeavours, especially the written word, will be successful.

FRIDAY, 29TH OCTOBER
Moon opposite Mars

Your mood is dreamy and distant today. You want to disconnect yourself from the world and all its demands and responsibilities. Unfortunately, an opposition between the Moon and Mars in the work sector of your chart today will make this impossible to achieve. Keep your nose to the grindstone, your shoulder to the wheel and your best foot forward. Later in the day, you can lay whatever is left of your body down for a nice rest.

SATURDAY, 30TH OCTOBER
Mercury into Sagittarius

Mercury moves into a part of your horoscope that is concerned with creativity. Mercury rules such things as thinking, learning and communications, but it can also be associated with skills and craftwork of various kinds. The combination of creativity and craftwork suggests that the next few weeks would be a good time to work on hobbies such as dressmaking, carpentry and so on.

SUNDAY, 31ST OCTOBER
Moon square Sun

Nostalgia and more than a touch of insecurity mingle as the Moon enters a stressful aspect with the Sun today. You need some reassurance that your domestic and emotional life is safe and lasting. Any hint of change will be disturbing today so stick close to home and don't overload your schedule.

November at a Glance

LOVE	❤	❤	❤
WORK	★		
MONEY	£	£	£
HEALTH	☉	☉	
LUCK	♘	♘	

MONDAY, 1ST NOVEMBER
Void Moon

Today is one of those odd days when there are no important planetary aspects being made, not even to the Moon. The best way to tackle these kinds of days is to stick to your usual routine and to avoid starting anything new or tackling anything of major importance. If you do decide to do something large today, then it will take longer and be harder to cope with than it would normally.

TUESDAY, 2ND NOVEMBER
Moon square Mercury

You may not feel much like it but today you need to look into your financial situation and work out a sensible budget for the future. So get out those bank statements and look at your credit card statements and be honest with yourself before you find yourself right off the financial rails. You may feel like going out and enjoying yourself today, but duty calls and therefore it doesn't look as if you will achieve this.

LEO

WEDNESDAY, 3RD NOVEMBER
Moon trine Saturn

The aspect between the Moon and Saturn may not be exciting in any way, urging, as it does, hard work and redoubled efforts. However, you can do your income a lot of good by striving for excellence now. Your efforts will not go unnoticed by those who matter.

THURSDAY, 4TH NOVEMBER
Moon sextile Mercury

This could be a red-letter day! Letters, phonecalls and faxes could bring you great news. It might be worth making a small bet on something or other today because the planets seem to indicate some kind of windfall. This doesn't mean that you should put a large sum of money down on a wager because the planets are not that infallible. However, it may be worthwhile taking a chance with a very small amount.

FRIDAY, 5TH NOVEMBER
Moon trine Uranus

You seem to have a kind of magnetic attraction about you at the moment and it will be easy to catch the eye of anyone that you fancy. Someone may fall head over heels in love with you today, but even if they don't a nice flirtation would make an enjoyable alternative. Friends will want to be in your company and you should be the life and soul of any party.

SATURDAY, 6TH NOVEMBER
Sun opposite Saturn

There seems to be a change coming that will affect the most important areas of your life. For example, you may be looking at a change of direction at work or you may be seriously considering a move of house. Whatever this is, try not to act hastily but take your time to think things through and make the best decision for all concerned.

SUNDAY, 7TH NOVEMBER
Sun sextile Mars

This is a great day in which to get any outstanding chores out of the way, especially those connected with your own personal property or premises. This means, for instance, your home, your garage or any kind of shop or business premises that you own or that you are closely involved with. You may have to do something to help your parents too, and the day will end with you feeling tired but pleased with yourself.

LEO

MONDAY, 8TH NOVEMBER
New Moon
The New Moon falls in the sphere of home and family today indicating a need for a change. For some reason you've been dissatisfied with your domestic set-up so you may consider looking at house prices in your own or indeed another area. You probably feel that you need more space and light in your life that your present home isn't providing. A family member may be considering setting up home and deserves all the encouragement you can give.

TUESDAY, 9TH NOVEMBER
Mercury into Scorpio
If family life hasn't been a bed of roses recently, then Mercury's arrival in the area of home and family couldn't be at a more opportune time. For the next few weeks you'll be able to find the right way of approaching any domestic problems and sort them out with the minimum of fuss. Talking things over with those close to you will open hearts and minds in a way you would have thought impossible a few days ago. It's a good time to get in touch with more distant relatives too.

WEDNESDAY, 10TH NOVEMBER
Moon sextile Uranus
A pleasant surprise is the order of the day. You should treat your loved one to something luxurious. A spell at a beauty parlour or perhaps a relaxing massage would be a good idea.

THURSDAY, 11TH NOVEMBER
Moon trine Jupiter
With a good aspect between the Moon and Jupiter there should be a considerable easing in your emotional state. This is a day to breathe a sigh of relief, settle down into an aura of comfort and affection, and generally take it easy. Of course, you tend to be a stranger to quiet relaxation so involve yourself in an activity that you actually like. A day trip in company with one you love is a very good idea.

FRIDAY, 12TH NOVEMBER
Moon square Venus
This looks like a lethargic day. It's obvious that you've bitten off far more than you can chew in a work situation and are now suffering the after-effects. You won't want to be bothered with anything strenuous today.

LEO

SATURDAY, 13TH NOVEMBER
Moon conjunct Mars

It's a highly energetic and vital day as the Moon conjuncts Mars. It's fast and furious action all the way but at least you've got the physical strength and tenacity to cope with the pressure. In work, if you can keep your head while all around you are losing theirs, you won't be doing too badly at all.

SUNDAY, 14TH NOVEMBER
Saturn square Uranus

It's pretty certain that there'll be more than the usual number of frustrations today. The problem lies with Uranus which spurs you to action, and Saturn which tends to prevent it. You are likely to become quite irritable.

MONDAY, 15TH NOVEMBER
Moon square Saturn

It would be too easy to be gloomy today as your mood goes into a dip and takes everyone around you down with it! Pull yourself together for goodness' sake! Do something frivolous to lift yourself out of this pit of despondency.

TUESDAY, 16TH NOVEMBER
Mercury sextile Mars

You seem to be up to your neck in chores today and you may feel a bit swamped by them but if you ask your friends, family and neighbours to give you a hand, they will come to your rescue. The most helpful person will be a young male, possibly the son of a neighbour, who would be glad to help out and even more glad if there was a bit of pocket money in it for him. Ask your partner to give you a hand too.

WEDNESDAY, 17TH NOVEMBER
Venus sextile Pluto

This is a wonderful day in which to get together with your lover and discuss whatever is on your minds. You will soon come to the conclusion that you feel exactly the same way as each other about the most important aspects of your lives.

THURSDAY, 18TH NOVEMBER
Moon trine Mercury

There is a highly charged atmosphere around you just now and this is forcing you to look at your home situation and also your joint financial arrangements. Today's excellent aspects between the Moon and Mercury suggest that you will be able to talk over some of your worries with those you are close to. It may be a good idea to chat about joint financial matters while you are about it too.

FRIDAY, 19TH NOVEMBER
Moon sextile Neptune

It's a great day to plan an outing with a loved one. A break away from routine would do you both the world of good so get down to the travel agents and book a holiday.

SATURDAY, 20TH NOVEMBER
Venus trine Uranus

You may be suddenly smitten by Cupid's arrow today, because the planets are tugging your emotions first one way and then another. You seem to be particularly vulnerable to sudden infatuations and it may be hard for you to keep your head while in this strange mood. A friend may be instrumental in introducing you to a fascinating new person who turns your heart on its axis.

SUNDAY, 21ST NOVEMBER
Mars square Jupiter

It's obvious that you've had your sights lifted out of a rut but that's no reason to let your new-found insight go to your head. The world seems a marvellous place just now, but don't be fooled into thinking that universal harmony will just happen of its own accord. Keep your feet on the ground. Be optimistic by all means, but going over the top about it isn't doing anyone any favours.

MONDAY, 22ND NOVEMBER
Sun into Sagittarius

You are going to be in a slightly frivolous frame of mind over the next few weeks and you shouldn't punish yourself for this. Pay attention to a creative interest or a demanding hobby now or get involved in something creative on behalf of others. A couple of typical examples would be to be the production of a school play or making preparations for a flower and vegetable show.

TUESDAY, 23RD NOVEMBER
Full Moon

Today's Full Moon could make you feel a bit tetchy and tense and it could also bring you some sort of unexpected expense. The best thing to do today is to stick to your usual routine and not start anything new or important. Jog along as usual and try not to become caught up in anybody else's bad mood now.

WEDNESDAY, 24TH NOVEMBER
Moon trine Venus

A chat with a woman friend may be just the thing to help you get things into perspective today. You seem to need some kind of practical advice in order to prevent you from taking a rather foolish course of action. A pal may suggest an unexpected and rather unusual outing later in the day and you would be missing a lot of fun if you turned this down.

THURSDAY, 25TH NOVEMBER
Sun sextile Neptune

If your love life has been a bit dull lately, today's events should cheer things up. Your personal charisma is really high at the moment and this should encourage any number of fascinating men or women to take an interest in you. Whether you simply enjoy a terrific flirtation or whether you deepen your relationship with the partner you are already with, you will enjoy it.

FRIDAY, 26TH NOVEMBER
Mars into Aquarius

Today, Mars moves into the area of your chart that is devoted to relationships. This planetary situation is like a double-edged sword because, on the one hand, it could bring you closer to your partner or loved one while, on the other hand, it can cause you to become extremely angry at the behaviour of others.

SATURDAY, 27TH NOVEMBER
Moon opposite Neptune

Your other half may be off in a fantasy world today, and it will do no good in trying to tempt him or her back down to earth. Eventually cloud-cuckoo land will lose its appeal but you'll have to be patient until then!

SUNDAY, 28TH NOVEMBER
Moon square Mercury

There will be a number of ups and downs today which will have your emotions swinging from one extreme to another. Someone may say something that really upsets you and, worse still, makes you doubt yourself. If you talk this over with a friend or a relative, you will find that they are just as outraged as you are at the unpleasant way you have been treated. It's nice to find out who your friends are.

MONDAY, 29TH NOVEMBER
Mars conjunct Neptune

Passions unite with sensitivity under today's stars. Neptune and Mars combine to bring that rarest of all things a tender, yet forceful expression of love. Men in your life will be exactly as you desire them to be. In close relationships especially, your lover will have an instinctive understanding of your desires.

TUESDAY, 30TH NOVEMBER
Moon trine Saturn

Your patience and capacity for hard work are needed to make the best of today. The hard taskmaster Saturn is to blame for all the effort you have to put in, but at least there is the promise of a well-earned financial reward at the end of it.

December at a Glance

LOVE	❤				
WORK	★	★	★	★	
MONEY	£				
HEALTH	✚	✚	✚	✚	✚
LUCK	♘	♘	♘	♘	♘

WEDNESDAY, 1ST DECEMBER
Venus opposite Jupiter

It's too easy to tempt you with forbidden delights today. Jupiter and Venus are playing on your weaknesses now and you're not only likely to give in, but to embrace your failings. Diets and resolutions such as giving up smoking are set to suffer from your weak-willed attitude. But, then again, it is said that a little of what you fancy does you good. Just don't go over the top.

THURSDAY, 2ND DECEMBER
Moon sextile Sun

A woman may have some surprising news for you today and, fortunately, it looks as if the news is likely to be good. Children may surprise you in a particularly pleasant way today too.

FRIDAY, 3RD DECEMBER
Moon opposite Jupiter

It's a very restless day as the Moon opposes Jupiter. You're likely to feel bored and stifled by the familiar now and yearn for a little adventure. Travel may be fraught with delays though, so it may be wisest to confine yourself to expanding your knowledge via reading rather than risking a traffic jam.

SATURDAY, 4TH DECEMBER
Moon square Neptune

You are likely to be nagged today, but even so you won't be in the mood to do very much or to follow anyone else's instructions. You could do with some peace and quiet to potter around the home. We just hope you get the chance!

SUNDAY, 5TH DECEMBER
Venus into Scorpio

Old scores and family squabbles can now be laid to rest as the passage of Venus into your domestic area signals a time of harmony and contentment. Surround yourself with beauty, both in terms of affection and in material possessions. This is a good time to renew a closeness with those you love. Join forces to complete a major project such as redecoration, or even a move of home itself. Be assured that the stars smile on you now.

MONDAY, 6TH DECEMBER
Sun sextile Uranus

Friends will surprise you in the nicest possible way today. Single people who are reading this may suddenly discover that someone whom you considered as nothing more than a buddy is becoming far more important to you now. A friend could introduce you to someone wonderful today too. Alternatively, a friend could simply show you that they appreciate your friendship.

TUESDAY, 7TH DECEMBER
New Moon

There's a New Moon today casting a glow over your artistic potential. Your talents should shine now so have some belief in yourself and in what you can offer to the world at large. If art and literature leave you cold, you may be more inclined to an amorous path. Conventional values are not for you now since you're determined to be yourself and to chart your own course. Make time to have fun, you deserve it.

WEDNESDAY, 8TH DECEMBER
Venus square Neptune

You are too sentimental for your own good today. The most unlikely event will remind you of things long ago, but some of them would be best forgotten!

Try to keep some sense of reality now, because you aren't very logical or practical today.

THURSDAY, 9TH DECEMBER
Moon sextile Venus

Certain domestic jobs are just too large to be carried out alone, so you'll have to rope in a family member to give you a helping hand. Many hands make light work as they say, and this shared effort could help you reach a renewed understanding with someone who has been a disruptive force within your family circle.

FRIDAY, 10TH DECEMBER
Mars square Saturn

Some worries in your partner's life will show up as nervous tension and irritability today. You're quite likely to blame yourself for all sorts of imagined ills. Leave your lover to his or her own devices and wait until they are back to a more reasonable frame of mind. A short trip might do the trick.

SATURDAY, 11TH DECEMBER
Mercury into Sagittarius

Serious concerns should be the last thing on your mind as Mercury enters your Solar house of fun and leisure from today. Jokes, witty quips and a display of eloquence will make you one of the most popular people around. Creatively speaking, Mercury also enhances more general powers of communication so you should consider setting down your thoughts in a lasting form. Creative writing whether prose or poetry would fulfil an instinct to express your talents.

SUNDAY, 12TH DECEMBER
Mercury sextile Neptune

The atmosphere inspires love today. Mercury ensures that you will be charming and attractive while Neptune gives you the insight and sympathetic understanding to make a success in love.

MONDAY, 13TH DECEMBER
Moon sextile Sun

This is a good time for your love life. If you are deeply committed, then you should share quality time with your partner. If single, then today could bring you into contact with someone who will become very important romantically.

LEO

TUESDAY, 14TH DECEMBER
Mars conjunct Uranus

It's a day of surprises, but thankfully they are likely to be good ones. In contrast to the usual disruptive influences of Uranus and Mars, conflicts could end now. A gesture of affection like the sudden arrival of a bunch of flowers could make everything in your relationship garden bloom again.

WEDNESDAY, 15TH DECEMBER
Venus opposite Saturn

Events are conspiring to make you choose between various sides of your life now. For example, you may be offered a wonderful job that represents a real opportunity for you but it may mean relocating or leaving your parents or other support groups behind. On the other hand, your home and family may be needing your attention, thus making it difficult for you to pursue your career aims for the time being.

THURSDAY, 16TH DECEMBER
Moon sextile Neptune

A close friend or partner will dream of faraway places and exotic holidays today. Why not look into the possibilities? You may not end up anywhere half as romantic in the end, but you'll still have a good time if you just had a change of scene!

FRIDAY, 17TH DECEMBER
Sun trine Jupiter

Anything that broadens your mind and gives new experiences is favoured by the Sun and Jupiter today. Travel is especially well starred and has a hint of romance involved with it. However, learning something for the pure joy of knowledge is also part and parcel of today's stars.

SATURDAY, 18TH DECEMBER
Mercury conjunct Pluto

If you want to conceive a child, find the right school for one or make any kind of positive moves in connection with younger members of your circle, this is the day for it.

SUNDAY, 19TH DECEMBER
Moon conjunct Saturn

Though the going may be hard, you should keep your mind on the job and alert for any opportunities coming up. A person of authority will be well disposed towards you because all your hard work will be noticed and appreciated.

LEO

MONDAY, 20TH DECEMBER
Jupiter into Aries

The giant planet Jupiter changes sign today. It will remain in your area of distant travel and adventure for one year, in which time you can expand your mental and physical horizons and gain new life experiences. Educational, legal and all official affairs will be highlighted.

TUESDAY, 21ST DECEMBER
Moon opposite Pluto

There could be a conflict of some kind going on inside of your head today. For instance, your logical mind could be telling you one thing, while your intuition is telling you something completely different. In this case, follow your intuition by all means but don't lose sight of the logic of your situation. Try thinking things through when you are feeling less muddled.

WEDNESDAY, 22ND DECEMBER
Sun into Capricorn

The Sun moves into your Solar sixth house of work and duty for the next month. This Solar movement will also encourage you to concentrate on your health and well-being and also that of your family. If you are off-colour, the Sun will help you to get back to full health once again. If you have jobs that need to be done, the next month or so will be a good time to get them done.

THURSDAY, 23RD DECEMBER
Full Moon

The Full Moon in one of the most private sectors of your chart shows that a phase has come to an end. Many of the foibles and hang-ups you've known through your life must be reassessed now. If they don't have any useful purpose in your life, then you must be prepared to ditch them. Self-doubt and negative thinking are issues that should be addressed now. Believe in yourself for a whole new chapter in your life is about to open.

FRIDAY, 24TH DECEMBER
Venus square Mars

There's obviously trouble brewing when Venus and Mars are in such stressful aspect. This probably relates to a domestic issue that you and your partner can't see eye to eye about. What begins as a minor controversy could escalate into full-scale war if one or other doesn't back down. The best advice is to agree to differ and try to remember that it is Christmas!

SATURDAY, 25TH DECEMBER
Moon trine Pluto

It's going to be an emotional Christmas Day with all your feelings reaching a highly charged state. Romantically speaking, the object of your desire won't know what's hit him (or her). You're likely to sweep a loved on off their feet with the force of your passion. This could be a chance to overcome any obstacles within your relationship.

SUNDAY, 26TH DECEMBER
Mercury sextile Mars

You'll be a silver-tongued charmer today, with enough sex appeal to drive anyone wild with desire. You can use your seductive wiles to good advantage because no one could possibly resist you.

MONDAY, 27TH DECEMBER
Mercury trine Jupiter

Your thoughts will freely roam over the numerous possibilities that are open to you now. The two planets of the mind, Jupiter and Mercury, rule the day and urge you to question whether you've got the necessary qualifications to make your ambitions come true. Even if you aren't academically minded, there are plenty of new subjects to explore, either for fun or profit. Follow your curiosity today because it will lead you to where you ought to be! Travel affairs too should go particularly well now.

TUESDAY, 28TH DECEMBER
Moon square Mercury

Just because you are happy and finding life rather exciting, you shouldn't also neglect all those boring details that have to be dealt with. Try to keep some part of your mind on your job and also try not to allow your credit cards to have a life of their own. If you don't keep your feet on the ground now, you will be piling up problems for the future.

WEDNESDAY, 29TH DECEMBER
Moon square Sun

You may be operating perfectly well on an outer, worldly level but, underneath your cool and competent exterior, you could be feeling far less in control. Your parents may heap some kind of unwanted chore on you today and sisters and brothers who should be around to help out with this may disappear like snowballs when the sun comes out. Don't wear yourself out today if you can avoid it.

LEO

THURSDAY, 30TH DECEMBER
Mars sextile Jupiter

Happiness, optimism and adventure are the features of the day as Mars and Jupiter cast a marvellous aura over your chart. Seek out new experience, get out and about with your partner and open your eyes to a myriad of possibilities that await you. Unattached people may find that situation remedied.

FRIDAY, 31ST DECEMBER
Venus into Sagittarius

The last day of the century is a good time to begin new projects and to get great ideas off the ground. Venus is now moving into the area of your chart that is concerned with creativity, so over the next few weeks you can take advantage of this and get involved with some kind of creative process. Venus is concerned with the production of beauty, so utilize this planetary energy to enhance any of your creations now. Happy New Century!